MW00949261

INTRODUCTION

You're holding the key to unlocking the mysteries of the human body. Imagine learning about the muscular system by coloring each muscle, understanding its form and function.

Whether you are a student diving into the realms of biology, a healthcare professional seeking a refreshing review, or an anatomy enthusiast eager to unravel the secrets beneath the skin, our Anatomy Coloring Book offers a dynamic and hands-on approach to learning.

As you turn the pages and fill them with color, you'll find that the once-daunting task of understanding human anatomy becomes a fulfilling and enjoyable activity. This unique approach will not only solidify your knowledge but also awaken a deeper appreciation for the human body's beauty and complexity.

Danny Snyder is a visionary author who has improved the world of educational resources through his innovative approach to anatomy coloring books. With a profound passion for both art and science, Snyder embarked on a journey to bridge the gap between these seemingly disparate domains. His fascination with the intricacies of the human body, coupled with his artistic prowess, culminated in the creation of anatomy coloring books that not only educate but also captivate the minds of students, professionals, and enthusiasts alike.

Now, let's embark on this colorful exploration of the human body. Turn the page to Chapter 1, where we'll begin our journey with the building blocks of life: the cells. Get ready to dive into a world where learning meets creativity, and where the mysteries of the human body unfold in a spectrum of colors.

THE HUMAN CELL

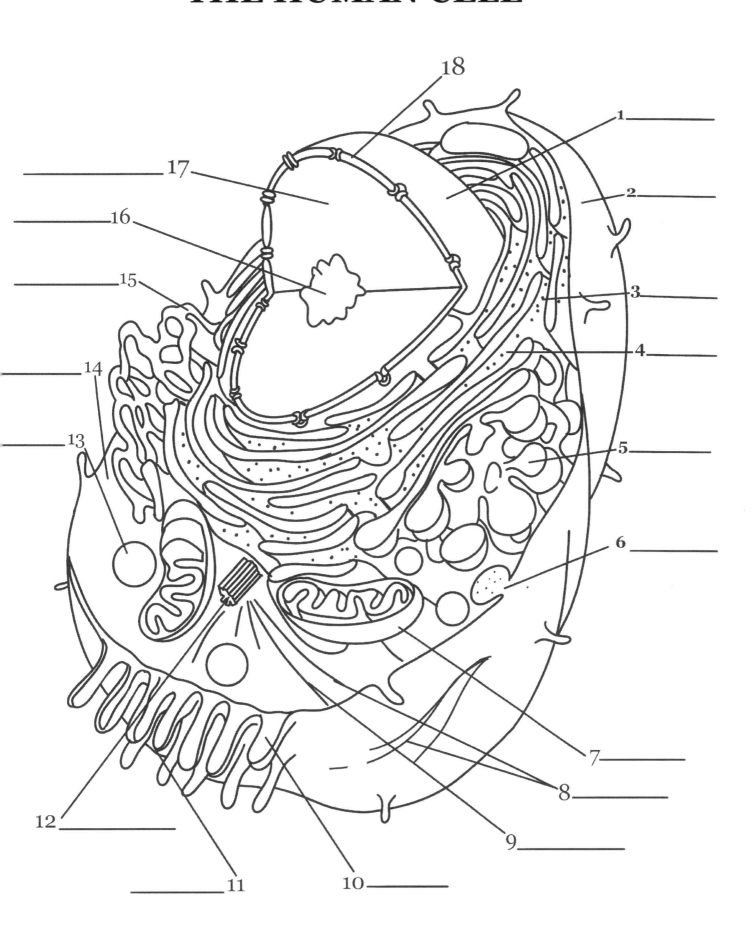

THE HUMAN CELL

1. Nucleus
2. Plasma Membrane
3. Rough Endoplasmic Reticulum
4. Ribosome
5. Golgi Apparatus
6. Exocytosis
7. Mitochondria
8. Intermediate Filaments
9. Microtubule
10. Microfilament
11. Microvilli
12. Centriole
13. Lysosome
14. Cytosol
15. Smooth Endoplasmic Reticulum
16. Nucleolus
17. Chromatin
18. Nuclear Envelope

FUN FACT

Cells are like tiny building blocks that make up living things, including our bodies. There are trillions of them in the human body. These cells give structure to the body, take in nutrients from food, turn those nutrients into energy

TYPES OF CELLS IN THE HUMAN BODY

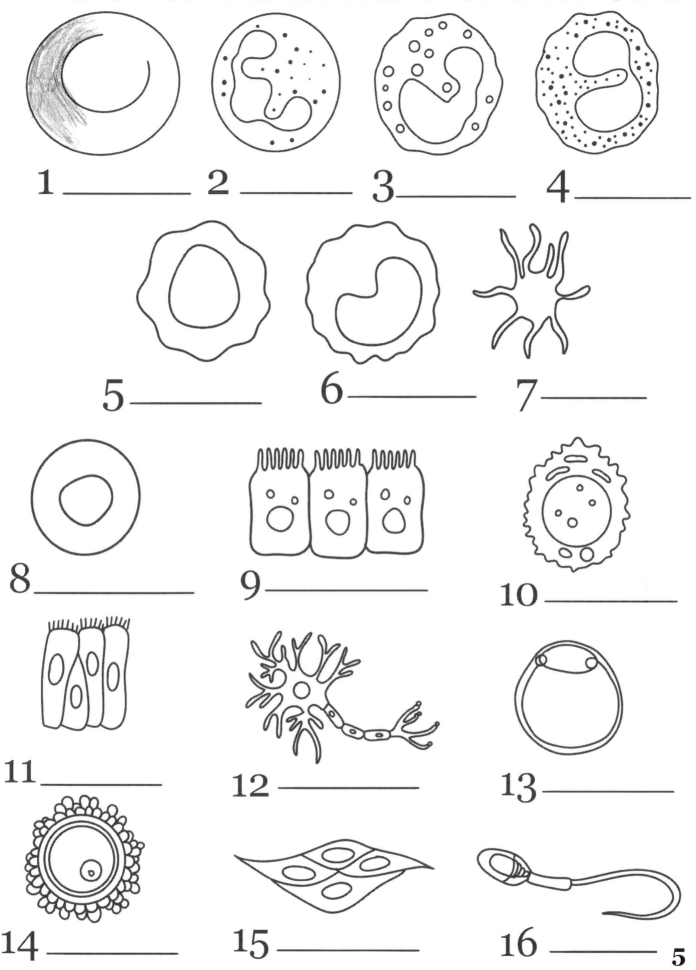

1 _____

2 _____

3 _____

4 _____

5 _____

6 _____

7 _____

8 _____

9 _____

10 _____

11 _____

12 _____

13 _____

14 _____

15 _____

16 _____

TYPES OF CELLS IN THE HUMAN BODY

1. RBC/Erythrocyte
2. Neutrophil
3. Basophil
4. Eosinophiles
5. Lymphocyte
6. Monocyte
7. Platelets
8. Stem cell
9. Intestinal cells
10. Chondrocyte
11. Epithelial cells
12. Neuron
13. Fat cell
14. Egg cell
15. Smooth muscle cell
16. Sperm cell

> **FUN FACT**
> Each cell in your body has its own set of identity cards called surface markers. These markers help the immune system recognize and distinguish between different cell types. It's like cells carrying their own passports

MUSCLE TYPES

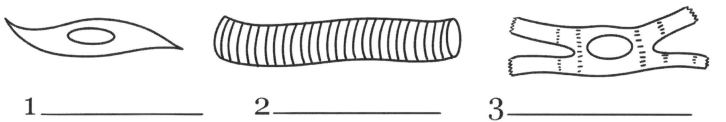

1 _____   2 _____   3 _____

Neuron Structure

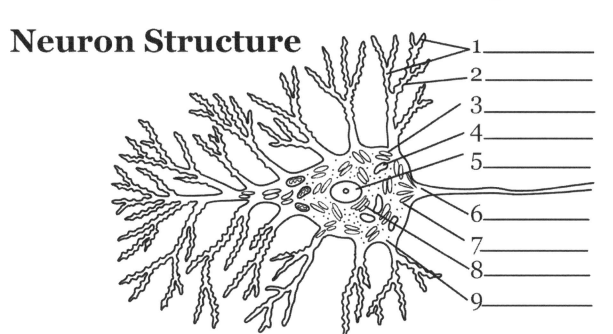

1 _____
2 _____
3 _____
4 _____
5 _____
6 _____
7 _____
8 _____
9 _____

Connective Tissue

10 _____
11 _____
12 _____
13 _____
14 _____
15 _____
16 _____
17 _____

1 _____
2 _____
3 _____
4 _____
5 _____
6 _____
7 _____
8 _____
9 _____

MUSCLE TYPES

1. Smooth Muscle
2. Skeletal Muscle
3. Cardiac Muscle

Neuron Structure

1. Dendrites
2. Dendritic spines
3. Rough endoplasmic reticulum (Nissl substance)
4. Mitochondria
5. Nucleus
6. Axon hillock
7. Neurotubules
8. Golgi body
9. Cell body of Neuron

Connective Tissue

1. Reticular fibers
2. Ground substance
3. Blood vessel
4. Fibroblasts
5. Eosinophils
6. Myofibroblasts
7. Mast cells
8. Lymphocytes
9. Neutrophils
10. Collagen fibers
11. Plasma cells
12. Macrophages
13. Lymphocytes
14. Mast cells
15. Macrophage
16. Adipocytes
17. Elastic fibres

SKELETON

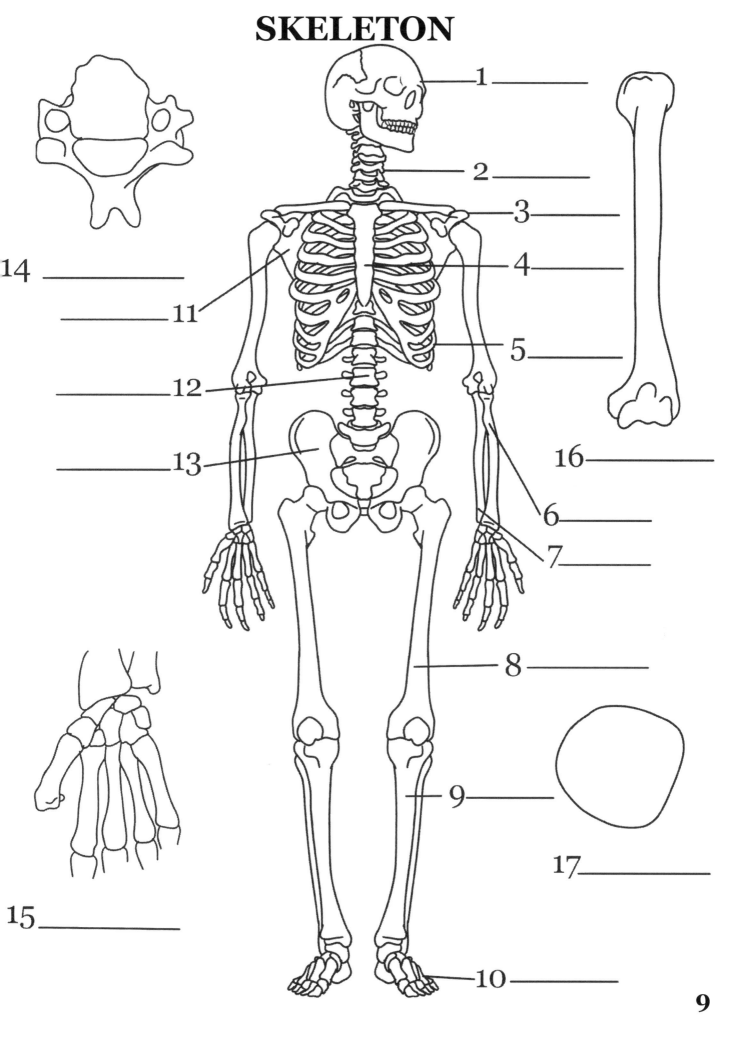

1 _____

2 _____

3 _____

4 _____

5 _____

14 _____

11 _____

12 _____

13 _____

16 _____

6 _____

7 _____

8 _____

9 _____

17 _____

15 _____

10 _____

9

SKELETON

1. Skull
2. Cervical vertebrae
3. Acromian process
4. Sternum
5. Riba
6. Radius
7. Ulna
8. Femur
9. Tibia
10. Metatarsals
11. Scapula
12. Lumbar vertebrae
13. Hip bone
14. Vertebrae
15. Wrist bones (carpals)
16. Humerus
17. Patella

FUN FACT

At birth, a human baby has around 270 soft bones. However, as they grow, some of these bones fuse together. By the time a person reaches adulthood, the number of bones in the human body is typically around 206. This process of bone fusion is why adults have fewer bones than infants

JOINTS

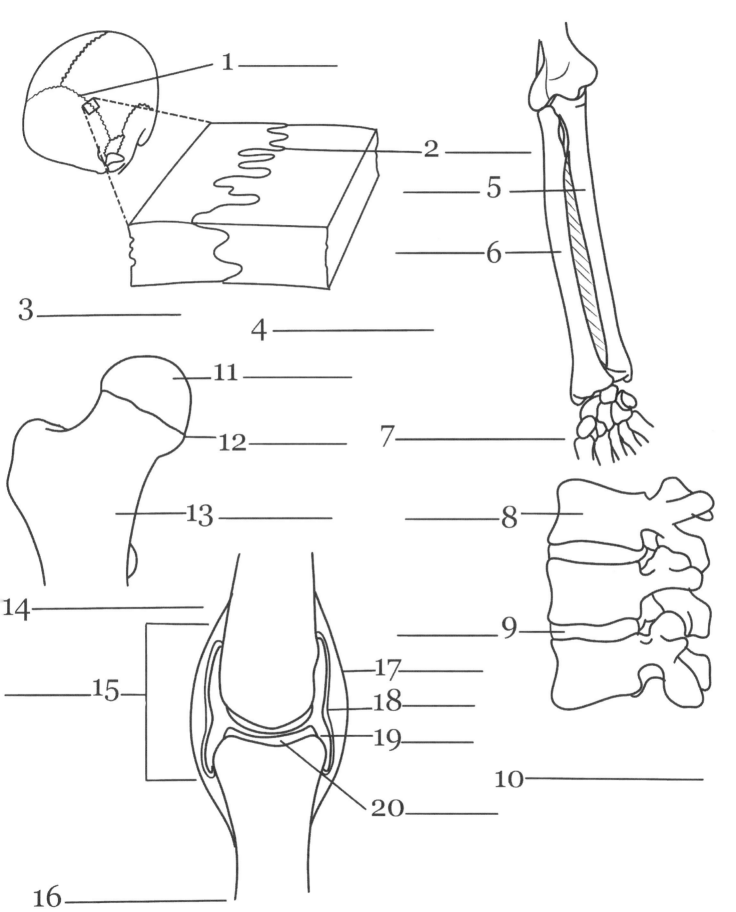

1

JOINTS

1. Coronal Suture
2. Suture
3. Synarthrosis (skull)
4. Fibrous joint
5. Ulna
6. Radius
7. Syndesmosis joint
8. Body of vertebra
9. Intervertebral disc
10. Secondary cartilaginous joint
11. Head of femur
12. Epiphysial plate
13. Femur
14. Primary cartilaginous joint
15. Synovial joint
16. Synovial joint
17. Fibrous capsule
18. Synovial membrane
19. Joint cavity
20. Articular cartilage

SKULL

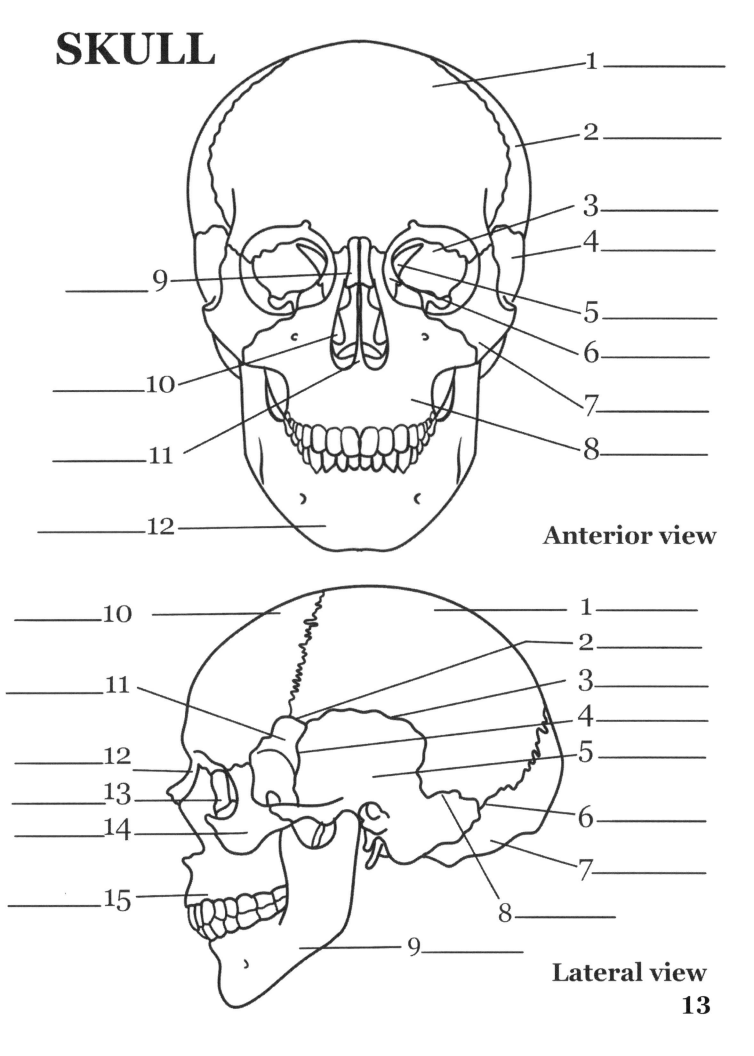

Anterior view

Lateral view

SKULL

Anterior view

1. Frontal
2. Parietal (paired bones)
3. Sphenoid
4. Temporal (paired bones)
5. Ethmoid
6. Lacrimal
7. Zygomatic
8. Maxilla
9. Nasal bone
10. Inferior nasal concha
11. Vomer
12. Mandible

Lateral view

1. Parietal bone
2. Sphenoparietal suture
3. Squamous suture
4. Spheno-squamous suture
5. Temporal
6. Occipitomastoid suture
7. Occipital bone
8. Parietomastoid suture
9. Mandible
10. Frontal
11. Sphenoid
12. Nasal
13. Lacrimal
14. Zygomatic
15. Maxilla

SKULL

Inferior view

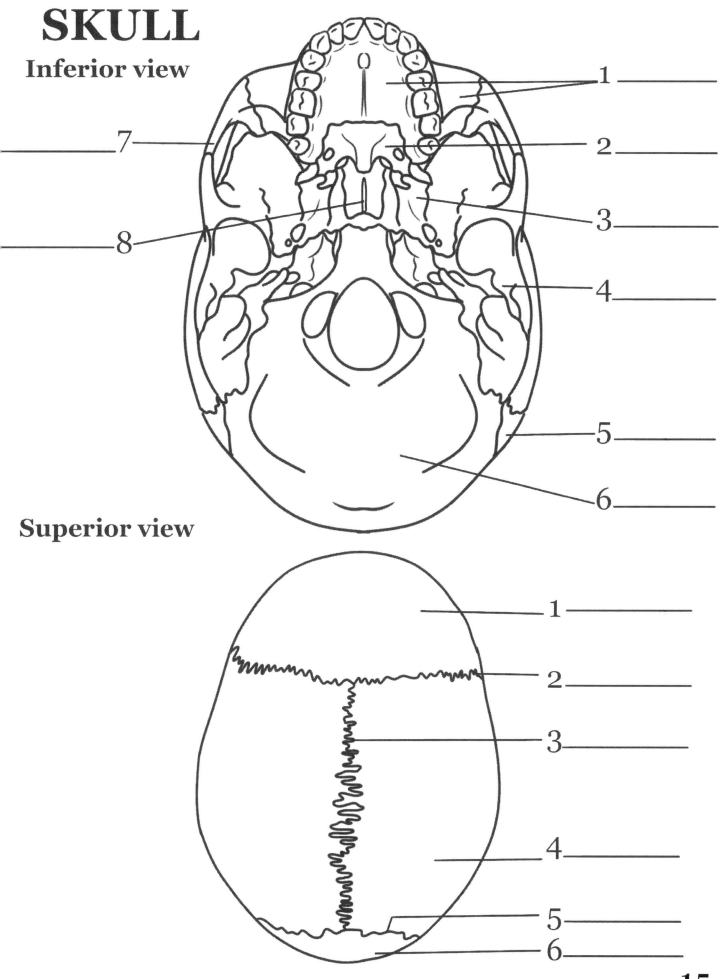

1

2

3

4

5

6

7

8

Superior view

1

2

3

4

5

6

15

SKULL

Inferior view

1. Maxilla
2. Palatine
3. Sphenoid
4. Temporal
5. Parietal
6. Occipital
7. Zygomatic
8. Vomer

Superior view

1. Frontal
2. Coronal suture
3. Sagittal suture
4. Parietal bone
5. Lambdoid suture
6. Occipital

FUN FACT

In newborns, the skull is not a solid mass of bone. Soft spots called fontanelles exist between the skull bones. These fontanelles allow for the flexibility needed during childbirth and also accommodate the rapid brain growth that occurs in infancy. Over time, these soft spots gradually close up as the bones fuse

VERTEBRAL COLUMN

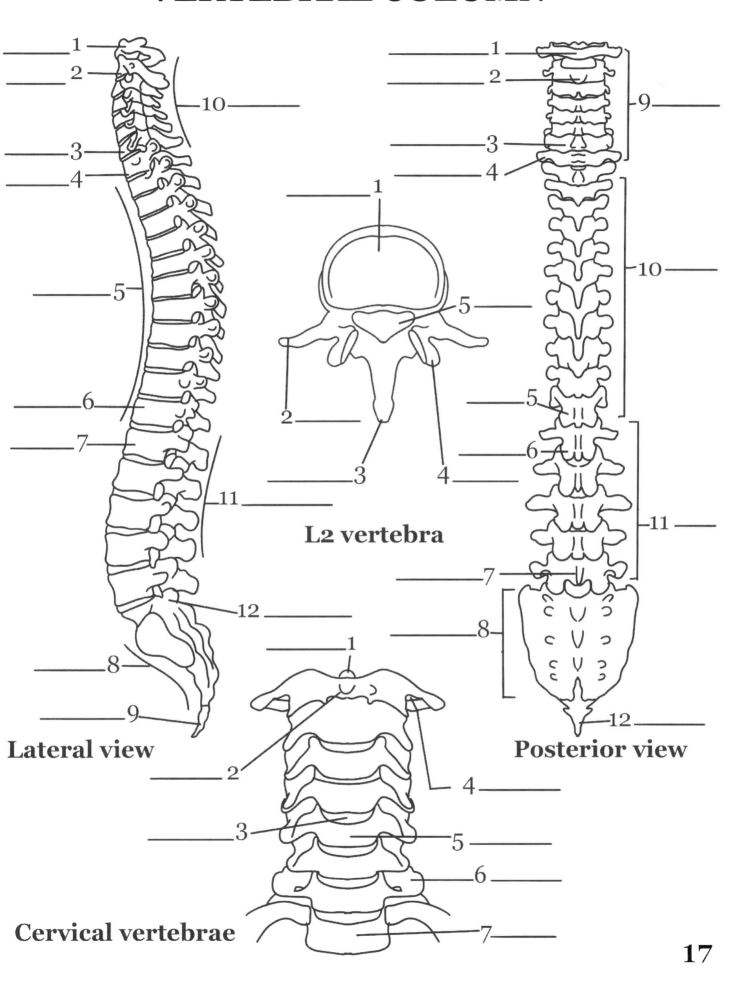

1
2
10
3
4
5
6
7
11
12
8
9

Lateral view

1
5
2
3
4

L2 vertebra

1
2
3
4
5
6
7

Cervical vertebrae

1
2
9
3
4
10
5
6
11
7
8
12

Posterior view

VERTEBRAL COLUMN

Lateral view

1. Atlas (C1)
2. Axis (C2)
3. C7
4. T1
5. Thoracic curvature
6. T12
7. L1
8. Sacral curvature
9. Coccyx
10. Cervical curvature
11. Lumbar curvature
12. Sacrum

L2 vertebra

1. Body
2. Transverse process
3. Spinous process
4. Articular facets
5. Vertebral foramen

Posterior view

1. Atlas (C1)
2. Axis (C2)
3. C7
4. T1
5. T12
6. L1
7. L5
8. Sacrum (S1–5)
9. Cervical vertebrae
10. Thoracic vertebrae
11. Lumbar vertebrae
12. Coccyx

Cervical vertebrae

1. Dens of the axis
2. Anterior tubercle of atlas
3. Intervertebral discs
4. Foramen transversarium
5. Body
6. Transverse process
7. First thoracic vertebra (T1)

FUN FACT

The spine has 33 vertebrae. Between them are cushion-like discs that act as shock absorbers. These discs, made of a gel-like center and a tough outer layer, absorb impact during activities like walking or running. This setup provides flexibility, prevents damage to the spine, and allows us to move and be active

THORACIC CAGE

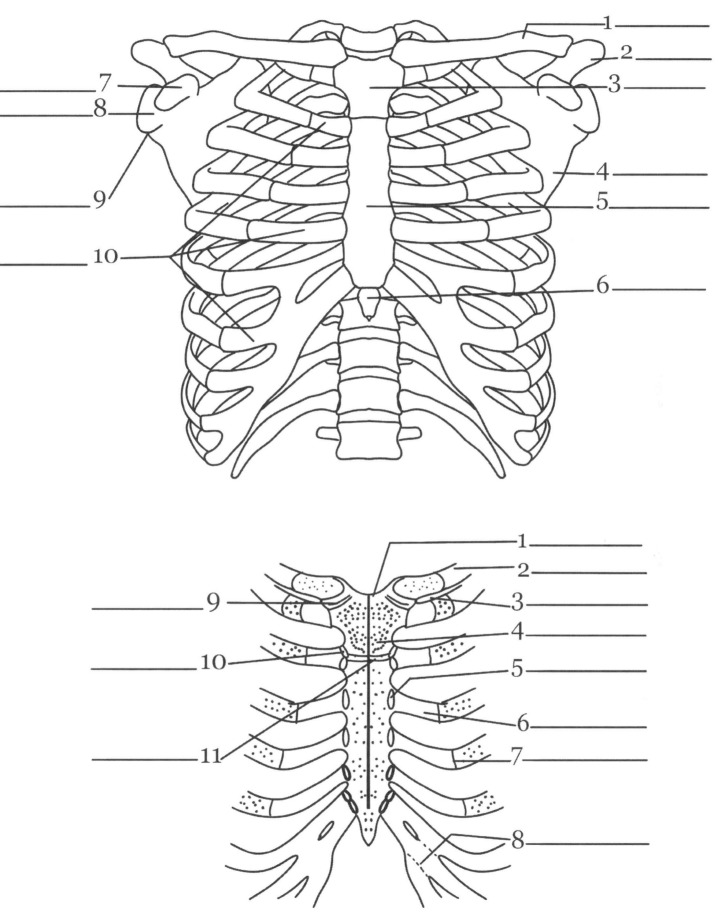

19

THORACIC CAGE

A.

1. Clavicle
2. Acromian
3. Manubrium
4. Subscapular fossa
5. Body of Sternum
6. Xiphoid process
7. Coracoid process
8. Genoid cavity
9. Neck
10. Costal cartilages

B.

1. Interclavicular ligament
2. Clavicle
3. Costoclavicular ligament
4. Manubrium
5. Articular cavity
6. Costal Cartilage
7. Costochondral joints
8. Interchondral joint
9. Articular disc
10. Intra-articular sternocostal ligament
11. Manubriosternal joint

PECTORAL GIRDLE

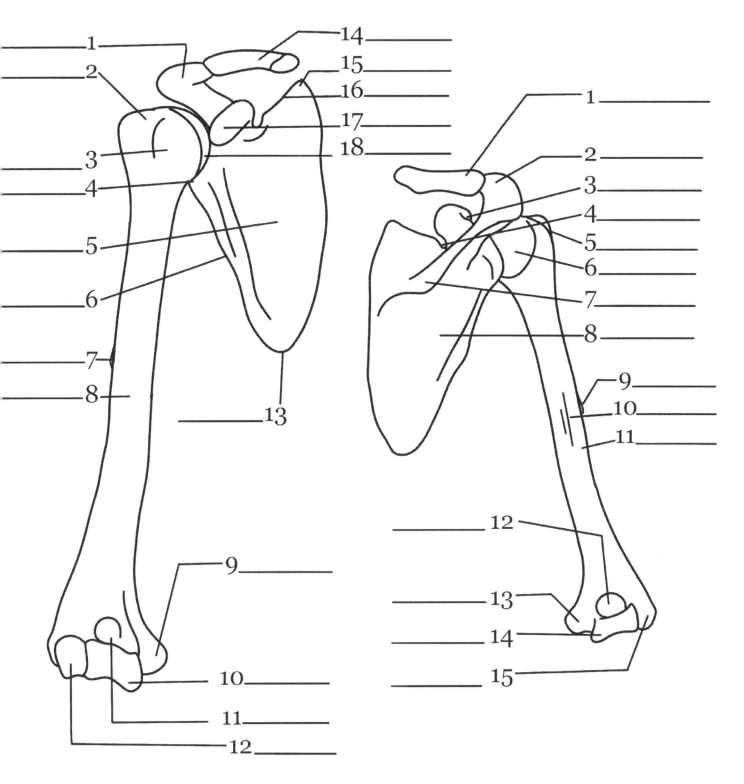

Anterior view

Posterior view

PECTORAL GIRDLE

Anterior view

1. Acromion
2. Greater tubercle
3. Lesser tubercle
4. Neck
5. Scapula
6. Lateral border
7. Deltoid tuberosity
8. Humerus
9. Medial epicondyle
10. Trochlea
11. Coronoid fossa
12. Capitulum
13. Inferior angle
14. Clavicle
15. Coracoid process of the scapula
16. Superior angle
17. Superior border
18. Head of femur

Posterior view

1. Clavicle
2. Acromion
3. Coracoid process
4. Supra- scapular notch
5. Greater tubercle
6. Head of humerus
7. Spine of the scapula
8. Scapula
9. Deltoid tuberosity
10. Radial groove
11. Humerus
12. Olecranon fossa
13. Medial epicondyle
14. Trochlea
15. Lateral Epicondyle

FOREARM,ELBOW JOINT AND HAND

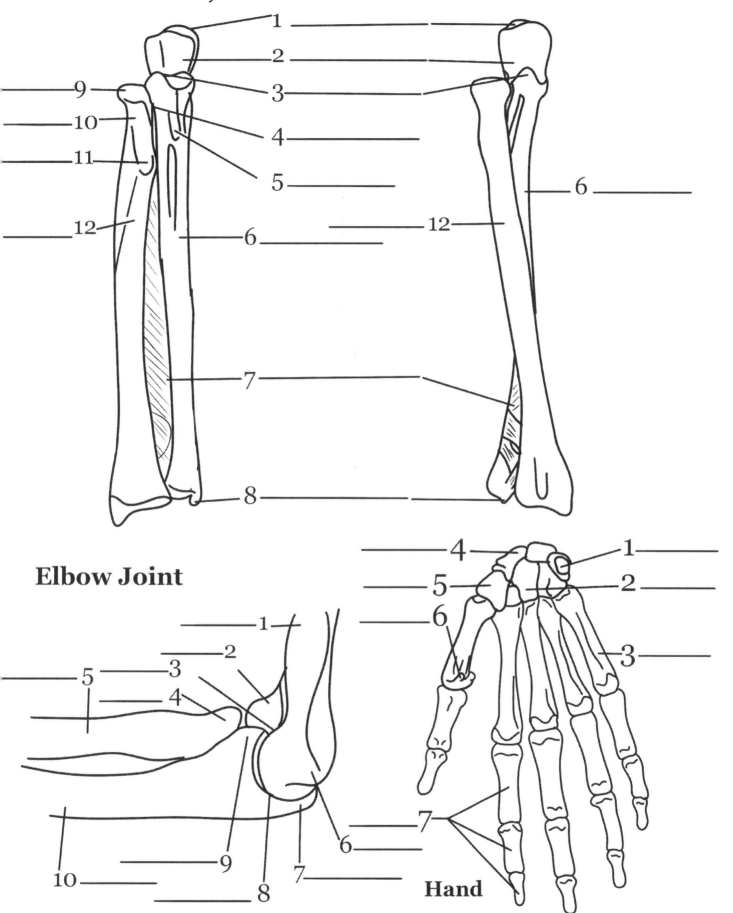

Elbow Joint

Hand

FOREARM, ELBOW JOINT AND HAND

1. Olecranon
2. Trochlear notch
3. Coronoid process
4. Radial notch of ulna
5. Ulna tuberosity
6. Ulna
7. Interosseous membrane
8. Styloid process of ulna
9. Head
10. Neck
11. Radial tuberosity
12. Radius

Elbow Joint

1. Humerus
2. Capitulum
3. Trochlea
4. Head Neck
5. Radius
6. Medial epicondyle
7. Olecranon
8. Trochlear notch
9. Coronoid process
10. Ulna

Hand

1. Pisiform
2. Capitate
3. Metacarpals
4. Scaphoid
5. Trapezium
6. Sesamoid bones
7. Phalanges

FUN FACT

In the forearm, there are two bones — the ulna and the radius. These bones are like buddies, working together to provide flexibility and support. When you rotate your forearm, the radius rolls over the ulna, allowing you to turn your hand palm up or palm down

PELVIC GIRDLE

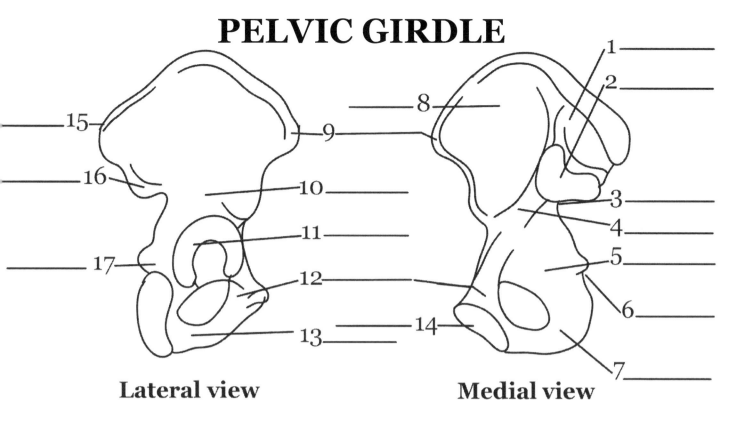

Lateral view   Medial view

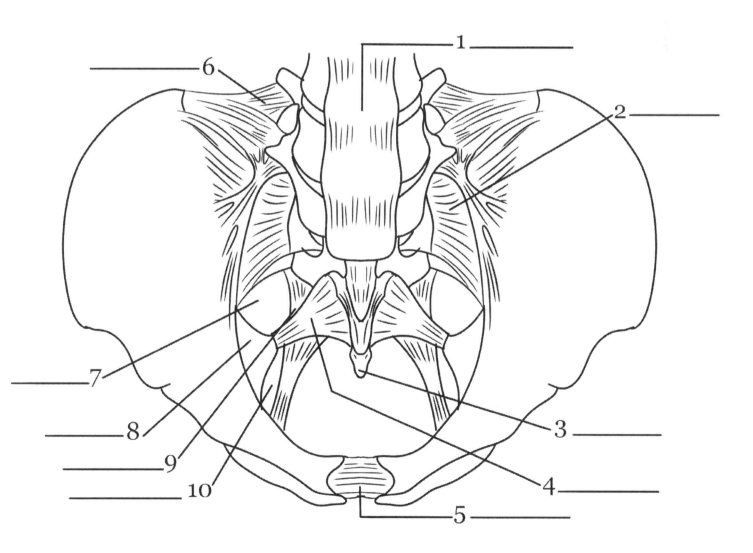

PELVIC GIRDLE

Medial & Lateral view

1. Iliac tuberosity
2. Auricular surface
3. Greater sciatic notch
4. Ilium
5. Ischium
6. Lesser sciatic notch
7. Ischial tuberosity
8. Iliac fossa
9. Anterior superior iliac spine
10. Ilium
11. Acetabulum
12. Pubis
13. Ramus of ischium
14. Pubic tubercle
15. Posterior superior iliac spine
16. Posterior inferior iliac spine
17. Ischium

FUN FACT

Your hip, also called the pelvic girdle, is like a puzzle made of three bones - the ilium, ischium, and pubis. These pieces start separate when you're a kid but gradually fit together as you grow up. By the time you're all grown, they create a strong foundation for your body, helping you stand, walk, and move comfortably

Anterior view

1. Anterior longitudinal ligament
2. Anterior sacro-iliac ligaments
3. Coccyx
4. Sacrospinous ligament
5. Pubic symphysis
6. Iliolumbar ligament
7. Greater sciatic foramen
8. Ischial spine
9. Sacrotuberous ligament
10. Lesser sciatic foramen

LOWER LIMB BONES

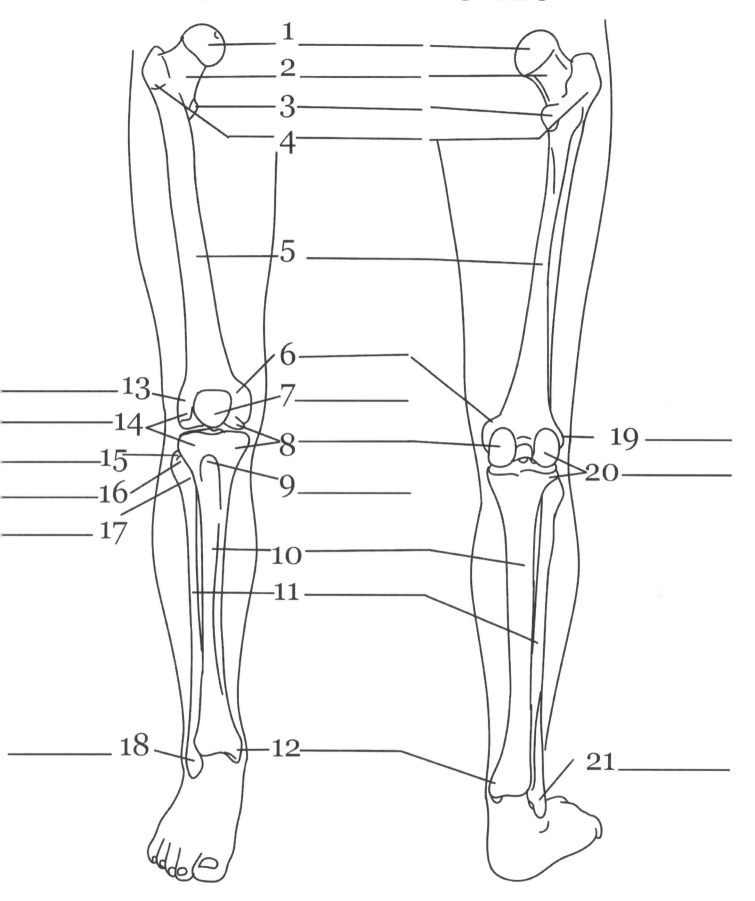

LOWER LIMB BONES

1. Head
2. Neck
3. Lesser trochanter
4. Greater trochanter
5. Femur
6. Medial epicondyle
7. Patella
8. Medial condyle
9. Tibial tuberosity
10. Tibia
11. Fibula
12. Medial malleolus
13. Lateral epicondyle
14. Lateral condyle
15. Apex
16. Head
17. Neck
18. Lateral malleolus
19. Lateral epicondyle
20. Lateral condyle
21. Lateral malleolus

FUN FACT

The kneecap, or patella, is like a helper for leg muscles. It sits in the front of the knee, working with the thigh muscles to make movements like walking and running smoother and more efficient

KNEE JOINT

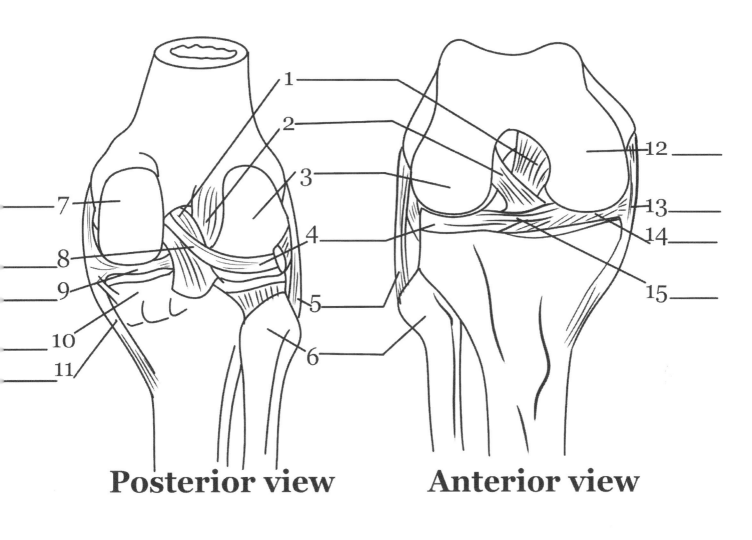

Posterior view   Anterior view

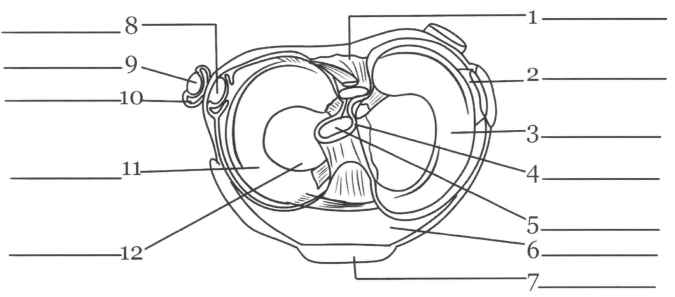

Superior view

KNEE JOINT

1. Posterior cruciate ligament
2. Anterior cruciate ligament
3. Lateral condyle of femur
4. Lateral meniscus
5. Fibular collateral ligament
6. Head of fibula
7. Medial condyle of femur
8. Posterior meniscofemoral ligament
9. Medial meniscus
10. Medial condyle of tibia
11. Tibial collateral ligament
12. Medial condyle of femur
13. Medial collateral ligament
14. Medial meniscus
15. Transverse Ligament

Superior view

1. Posterior cruciate ligament
2. Medial collateral ligament
3. Medial meniscus
4. Synovial membrane
5. Anterior cruciate ligament
6. Infrapatellar fat pad
7. Patellar ligament
8. Popliteus tendon
9. Lateral collateral ligament
10. Bursa
11. Lateral meniscus
12. Superior surface of tibia

FOOT BONES

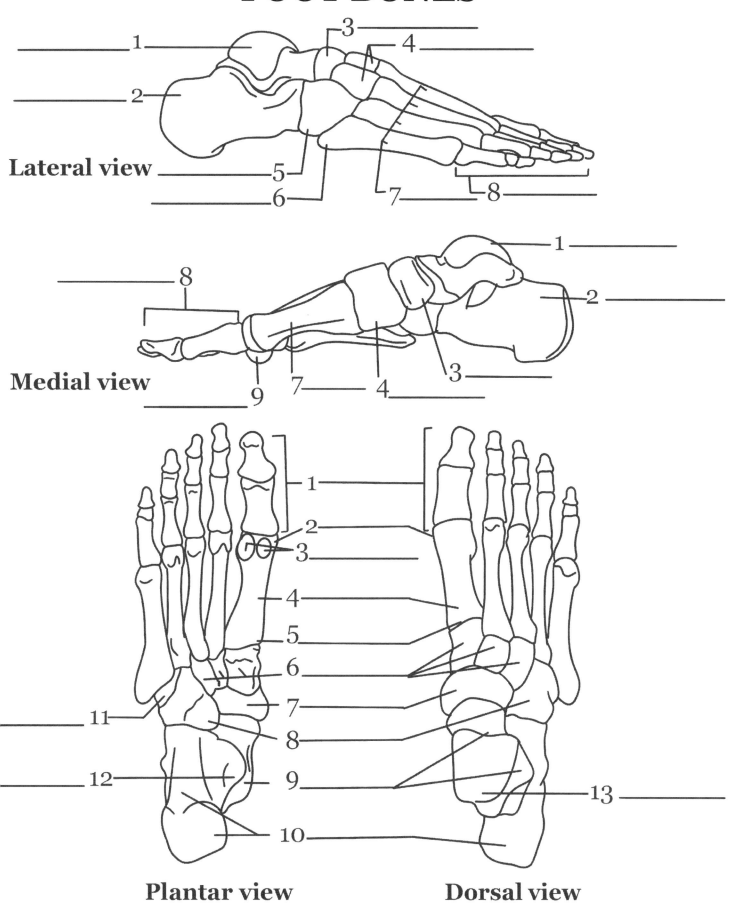

Lateral view

Medial view

Plantar view

Dorsal view

FOOT BONES

Lateral & Medial View

1. Talus
2. Calcaneus
3. Navicular
4. Cuneiforms
5. Cuboid
6. Tuberosity of 5th metatarsal bone
7. Metatarsals
8. Phalanges
9. Sesamoid bone

Dorsal & Plantar view

1. Phalanges
2. Head
3. Sesamoid bone
4. Body
5. Base
6. Cuneiforms
7. Navicular
8. Cuboid
9. Talus
10. Calcaneus
11. Groove
12. Sustentaculum tali
13. Trochlea

FUN FACT

The foot has 26 bones, each playing a specific role. These bones form arches, acting like natural shock absorbers. The arches distribute our body weight, provide flexibility, and contribute to the foot's overall strength

FACIAL BONES

Lateral view

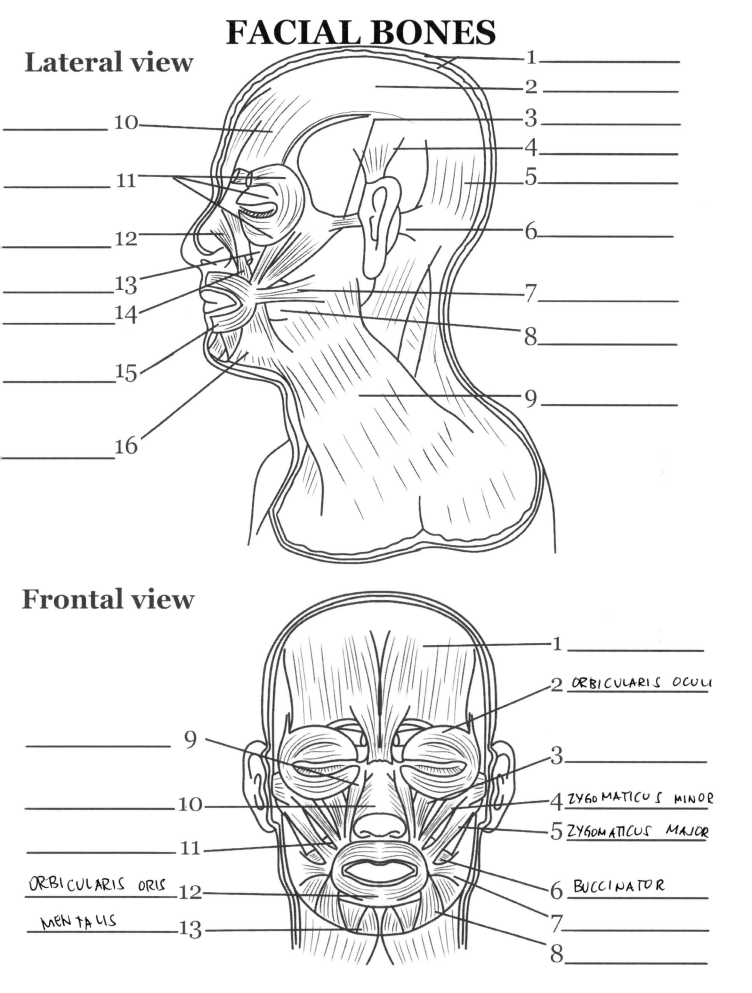

10 _____

11 _____

12 _____

13 _____

14 _____

15 _____

16 _____

1 _____
2 _____
3 _____
4 _____
5 _____
6 _____
7 _____
8 _____
9 _____

Frontal view

9 _____

10 _____

11 _____

ORBICULARIS ORIS 12

MENTALIS 13

1 _____

2 ORBICULARIS OCULI

3 _____

4 ZYGOMATICUS MINOR

5 ZYGOMATICUS MAJOR

6 BUCCINATOR

7 _____

8 _____

33

FACIAL BONES

Lateral view

1. Skin and subcutaneous tissue
2. Epicranial aponeurosis
3. Auricularis anterior muscle
4. Auricularis superior muscle
5. Occipitalis
6. Auricularis posterior muscle
7. Risorius
8. Buccinator
9. Platysma
10. Frontalis
11. Orbicularis oculi
12. Nasalis
13. Levator labii superioris
14. Levator labii superioris alaeque nasi muscle
15. Orbicularis oris
16. Depressor anguli oris

Frontal view

1. Frontalis
2. Orbicularis oculi
3. Levator labii superioris
4. Zygomaticus minor muscle
5. Zygomaticus major muscle
6. Buccinator
7. Risorius
8. Depressor labii inferioris muscle
9. Levator labii superioris alaeque nasi muscle
10. Nasalis
11. Levator anguli oris muscle
12. Orbicularis oris
13. Mentalis

MUSCLES OF THE PALATE AND TONGUE

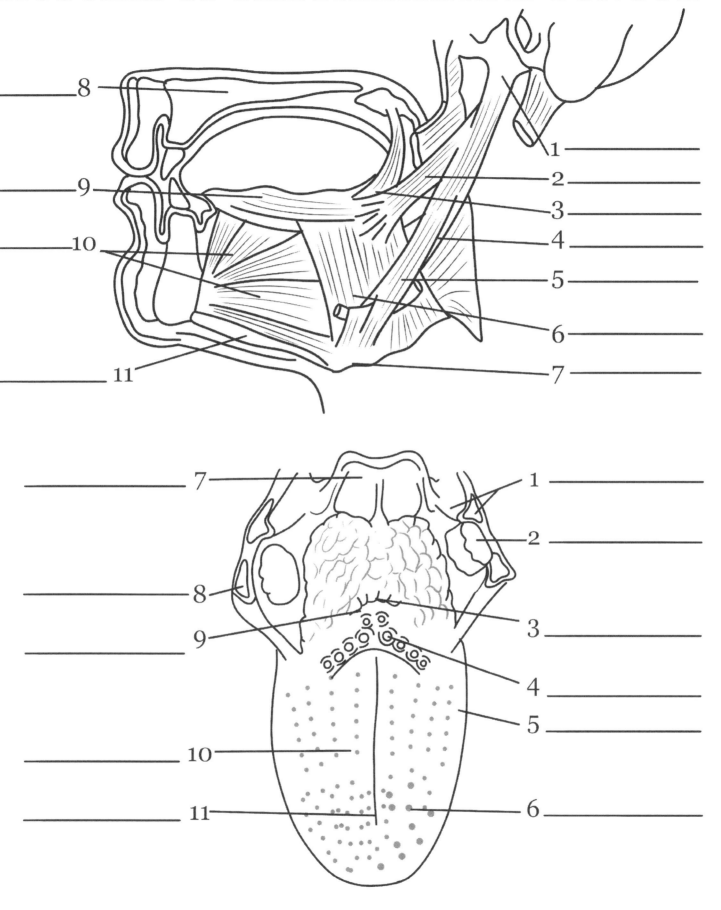

MUSCLES OF THE PALATE AND TONGUE

Palate

1. Styloid process
2. Styloglossus
3. Palatoglossus
4. Stylopharyngeus muscle
5. Stylohyoid muscle
6. Hyoglossus
7. Hyoid bone
8. Hard palate
9. Styloglossus
10. Genioglossus
11. Mylohyoid muscle

Tongue

1. Palatopharyngeal arch and muscle
2. Palatine tonsil
3. Foramen cecum
4. Vallate papillae
5. Foliate papillae
6. Fungiform papillae
7. Epiglottis
8. Palatoglossal arch and muscle
9. Terminal sulcus
10. Filiform papilla
11. Median sulcus

> **FUN FACT**
> Taste buds, located on the tongue's surface, detect different flavors: sweet, sour, salty, and bitter.
> The uvula, hanging down from the soft palate, aids in speech articulation and helps prevent food from entering the nasal cavity during swallowing

NECK MUSCLES

Lateral view

8 _____

9 _____

10 _____

STERNOCLEID MASTOID 11 _____

TRAPEZIUS 12 _____

1 _____

2 _____

3 _____

4 _____

5 _____

6 _____

7 _____

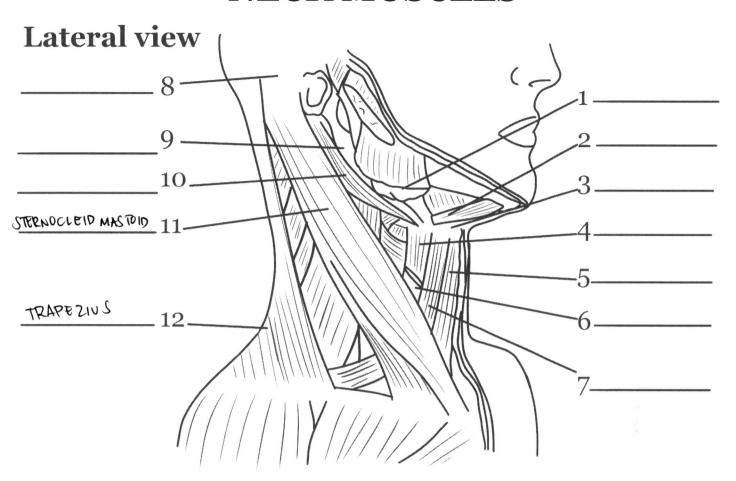

Anterior view

8 _____

9 _____

10 _____

11 _____

12 _____

13 _____

1 _____

2 _____

3 _____

4 _____

5 _____

6 _____

7 _____

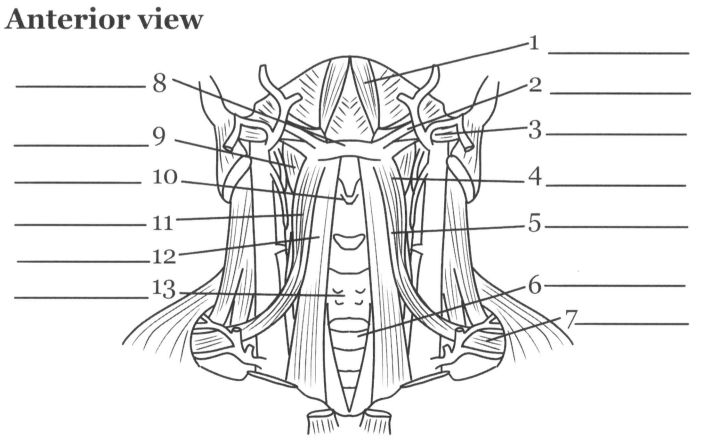

NECK MUSCLES

Lateral view

1. Submandibular gland
2. Anterior belly of the digastric
3. Hyoid bone
4. Thyrohyoid
5. Sternohyoid
6. Sternothyroid
7. Omohyoid
8. Mastoid process
9. Stylohyoid
10. Posterior belly of the digastric
11. Sternocleidomastoid
12. Trapezius muscle

Anterior view

1. Anterior belly of the digastric
2. Stylohyoid
3. Posterior belly of the digastric
4. Thyrohyoid
5. Sternothyroid
6. Trachea
7. Omohyoid
8. Hyoid bone
9. Thyrohyoid
10. Thyroid cartilage
11. Omohyoid
12. Sternohyoid
13. Thyroid cartilage

PREVERTEBRAL MUSCLES

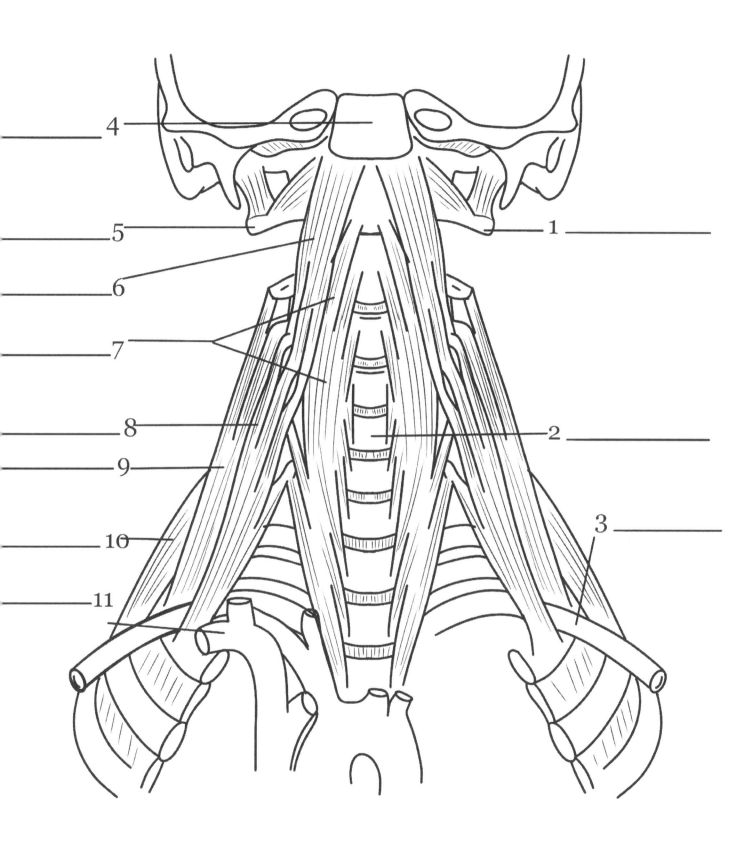

PREVERTEBRAL MUSCLES

1. Transverse process of atlas
2. Cervical vertebrae
3. Subclavian artery
4. Occipital bone
5. C1
6. Longus capitis
7. Longus colli
8. Anterior scalene
9. Middle scalene
10. Posterior scalene
11. Subclavian vein

FUN FACT

Prevertebral muscles play a crucial role in flexing the neck, tilting the head, and rotating the cervical spine. They contribute to the overall mobility and stability of the neck region

BACK MUSCLES

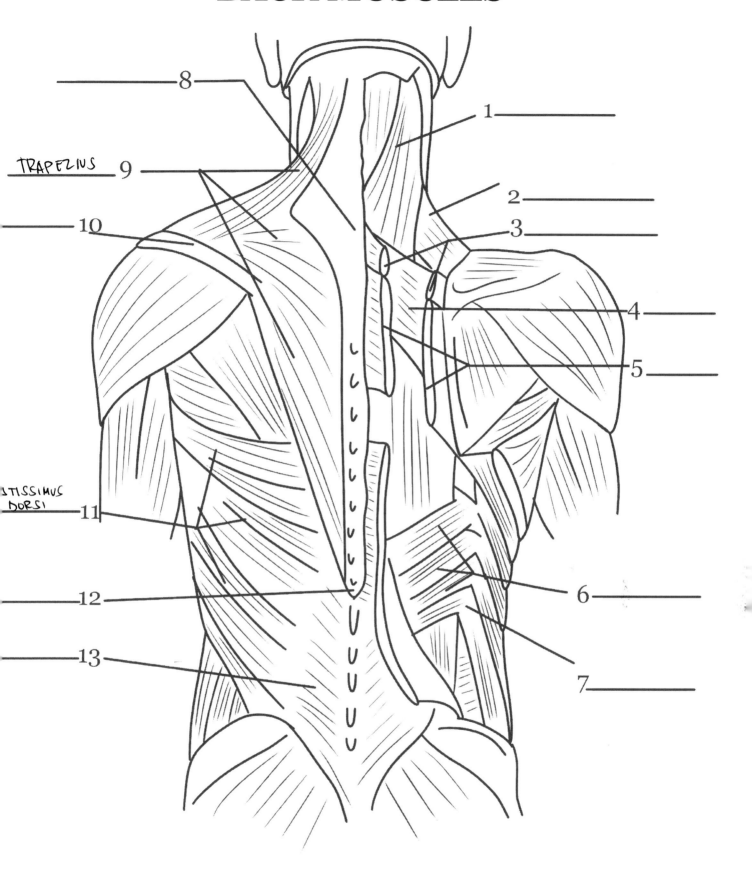

8

1

TRAPEZIUS 9

2

3

10

4

5

STISSIMUS DORSI

11

12

6

13

7

BACK MUSCLES

1. Splenius capitis
2. Levator scapulae
3. Rhomboid minor
4. Serratus posterior superior
5. Rhomboid major
6. Serratus posterior inferior
7. 12th rib
8. Spinous process of C7 vertebrae
9. Trapezius
10. Spine of Scapula
11. Latissimus dorsi
12. Spinous process of C7 vertebrae
13. Thoracolumbar fascia

FUN FACT

The trapezius muscles are shoulder elevators. They help you shrug your shoulders and move your head. The latissimus dorsi, or "lats," are the wide muscles that give your back a broad appearance

ANTERIOR ABDOMINAL WALL

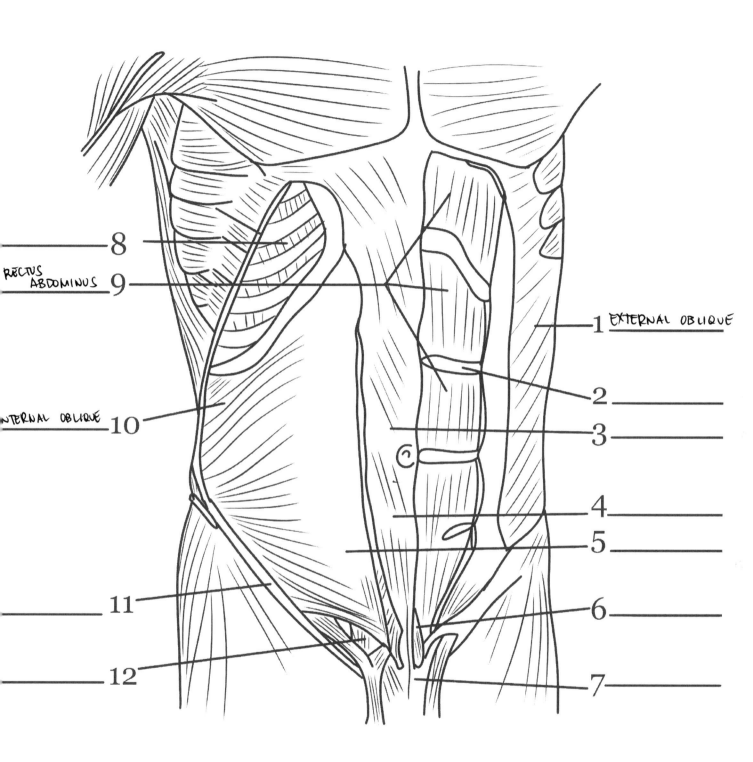

8

RECTUS
ABDOMINUS 9

EXTERNAL OBLIQUE 1

INTERNAL OBLIQUE 10

2

3

4

5

11

6

12

7

ANTERIOR ABDOMINAL WALL

1. External abdominal oblique
2. Tendinous intersection
3. Aponeurosis of external oblique muscle
4. Linea alba
5. Rectus sheath
6. Pyramidalis
7. Pubic tubercle
8. Intercostal muscles
9. Rectus abdominis
10. Internal abdominal oblique
11. Inguinal ligament
12. Conjoint tendon

FUN FACT

The front muscles in your belly, especially the one called rectus abdominis, can give you that cool "six-pack" look. The actual number of divisions can vary, and having visible ones is influenced by factors like genetics and body fat percentage

PELVIC MUSCLES

Female

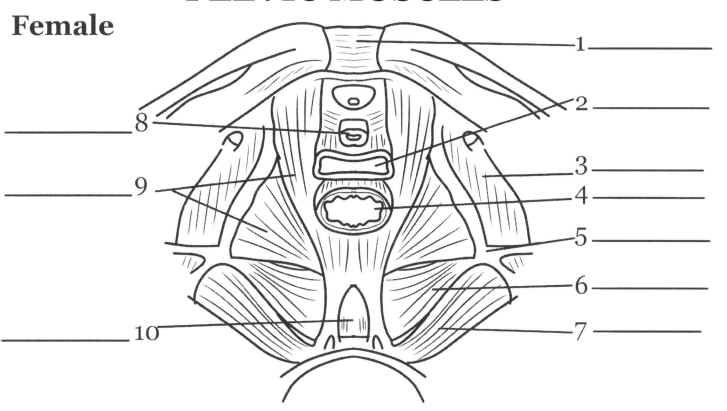

1
2
3
4
5
6
7
8
9
10

Male

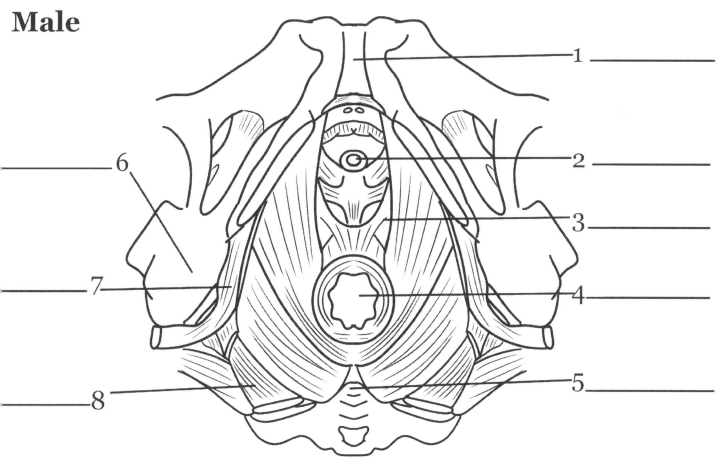

1
2
3
4
5
6
7
8

PELVIC MUSCLES

Female

1. Pubic symphysis
2. Vagina
3. Obturator internus
4. Rectum
5. Ischial spine
6. Coccygeus
7. Piriformis
8. Urethra
9. Levator ani
10. Coccyx

Male

1. Pubic symphysis
2. Urethra
3. Levator ani
4. Rectum
5. Coccyx
6. Ischial tuberosity
7. Obturator internus
8. Coccygeus

FUN FACTS

1) The pelvic floor muscles form a hammock-like structure at the base of the pelvis, providing crucial support for organs such as the bladder, uterus, and rectum.

2) As people age, pelvic floor muscles can weaken. This can lead to issues such as incontinence and pelvic organ prolapse

SHOULDER AND ARM MUSCLES

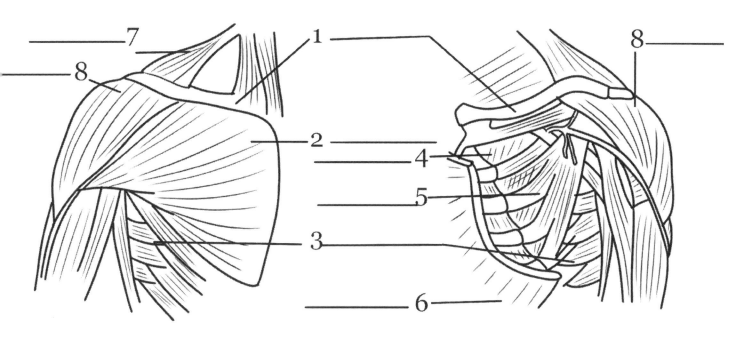

Superficial layer   ## Deep Layer

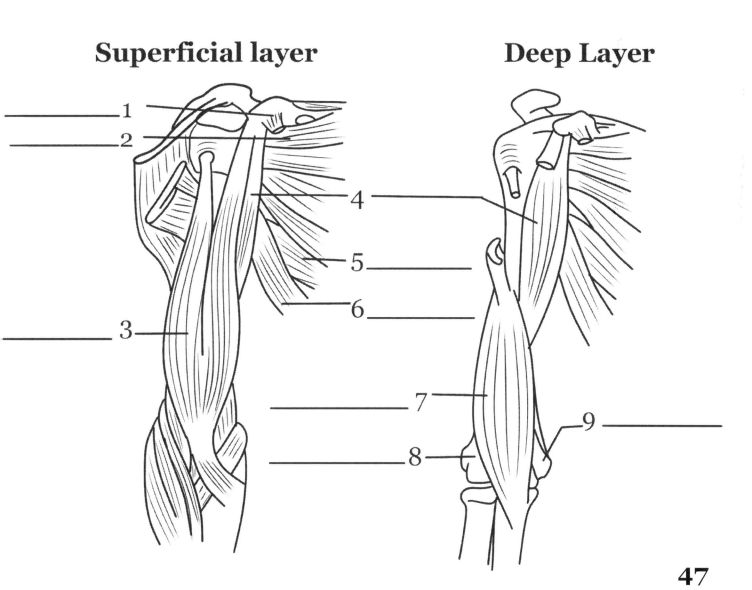

SHOULDER AND ARM MUSCLES

Shoulder

1. Clavicle
2. Pectoralis major
3. Serratus anterior
4. Subclavius
5. Pectoralis minor
6. Pectoralis major
7. Trapezius muscle
8. Deltoid

Arm Muscles

1. Coracoid process
2. Subscapularis muscle
3. Biceps brachii
4. Coracobrachialis
5. Teres major muscle
6. Latissimus dorsi muscle
7. Brachialis
8. Lateral epicondyle of humerus
9. Medial epicondyle of humerus

THIGH MUSCLES

Posterior view

Anterior view

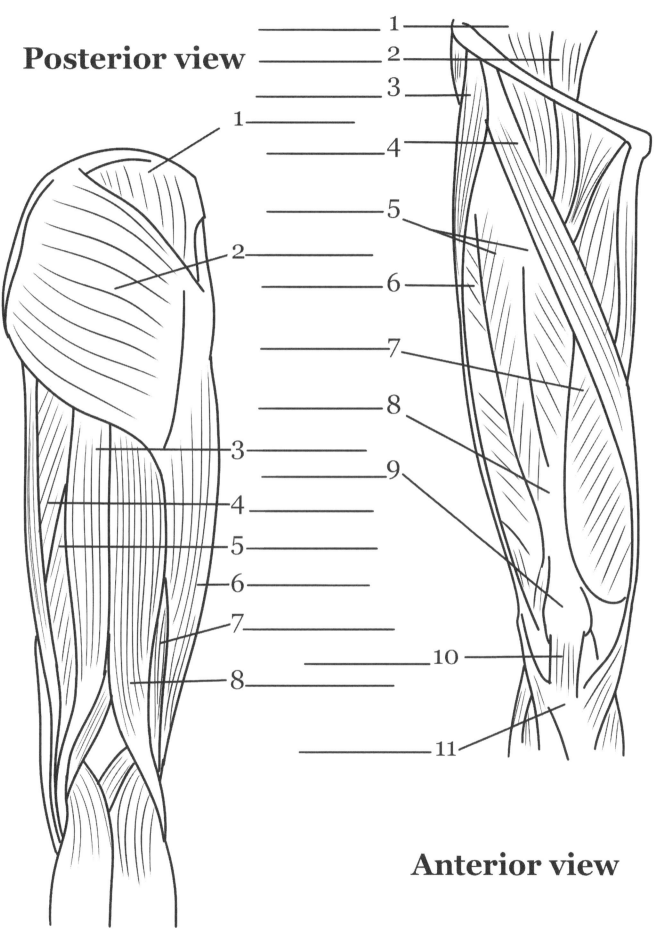

49

THIGH MUSCLES

Posterior view

1. Gluteus medius
2. Gluteus maximus
3. Semitendinosus
4. Adductor magnus muscle
5. Semimembranosus
6. Iliotibial tract
7. Biceps femoris, short head
8. Biceps femoris, long head

Anterior view

1. Psoas
2. Iliacus muscle
3. Tensor fasciae latae
4. Sartorius
5. Rectus femoris
6. Vastus lateralis
7. Vastus medialis
8. Quadriceps femoris tendon
9. Patella
10. Patellar ligament
11. Tibial tuberosity

FUN FACTS

The sartorius is the longest muscle in the human body. It runs diagonally across the thigh, enabling flexion, abduction, and external rotation of the hip.
Its name comes from the Latin word "sartor," meaning tailor, as it is often used when sitting cross-legged

LEG AND FOOT MUSCLES

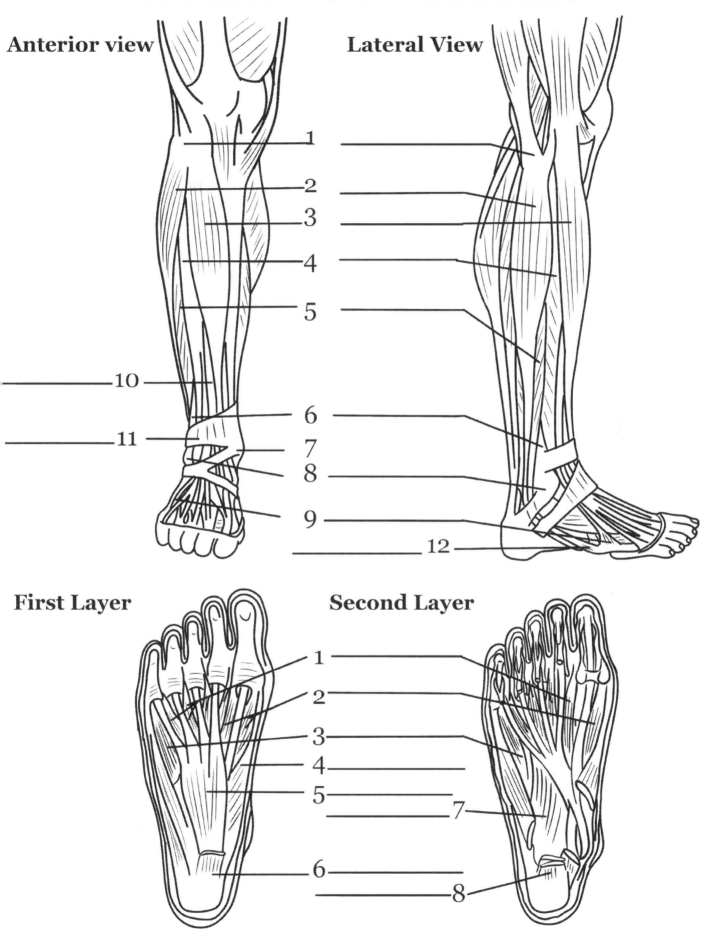

Anterior view

Lateral View

First Layer

Second Layer

LEG AND FOOT MUSCLES

Leg Muscles

1. Head of fibula
2. Fibularis longus
3. Tibialis anterior
4. Fibularis brevis
5. Extensor digitorum longus
6. Fibula
7. Medial malleolus
8. Lateral malleolus
9. Fibularis tertius
10. Extensor hallucis longus
11. Superior extensor retinaculum
12. Peroneus brevis tendon

Foot Muscles

1. Lumbricals
2. Flexor hallucis brevis
3. Flexor digiti minimi brevis
4. Abductor hallucis
5. Flexor digitorum brevis
6. Plantar aponeurosis
7. Quadratus plantae
8. Flexor digitorum brevis muscle

HEART

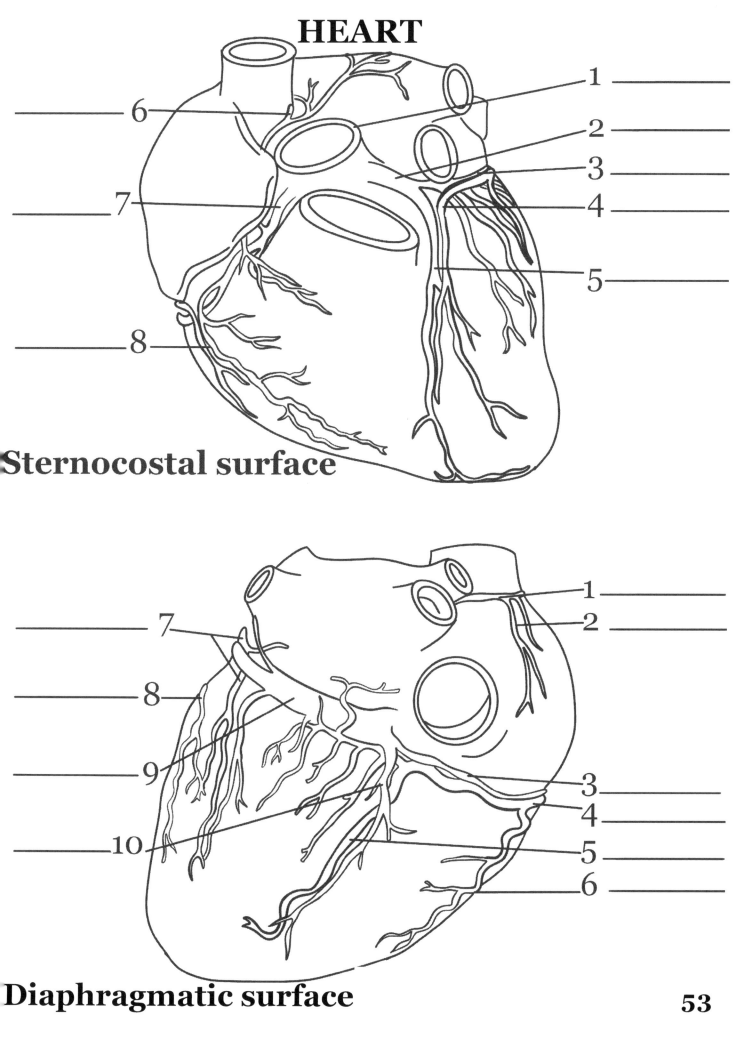

6

7

8

Sternocostal surface

1

2

3

4

5

7

8

9

10

1

2

3

4

5

6

Diaphragmatic surface

53

HEART

Sternocostal surface

1. Aorta
2. Left coronary artery
3. Circumflex branch of left coronary artey
4. Great cardiac vein
5. Anterior interventricular branch
6. SA nodal branch
7. Right coronary artery
8. Small cardiac vein

Diaphragmatic surface

1. SA nodal branch
2. SA node
3. Small cardiac vein
4. Right coronary artery
5. Posterior interventricular branch
6. Right marginal branch
7. Circumflex branch of left coronary artery
8. Left marginal branch
9. Coronary sinus
10. Middle cardiac vein

HEART AND PERICARDIUM

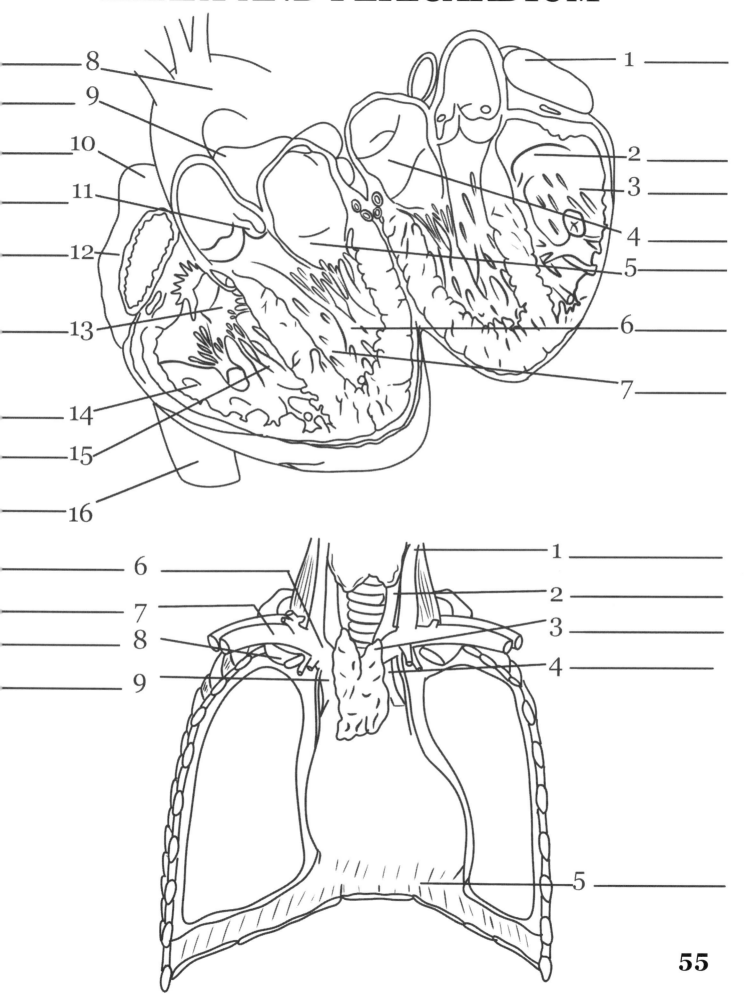

HEART AND PERICARDIUM

Heart

1. Right atrium
2. Pulmonary trunk
3. Right ventricle
4. Left atrium
5. Mitral valve
6. Papillary muscles
7. Left ventricle
8. Aortic arch
9. Pulmonary veins
10. Superior vena cava
11. Aortic semilunar valve
12. Right atrium
13. Tricuspid valve
14. Right ventricle
15. Papillary muscles
16. Inferior vena cava

Pericardium

1. Internal jugular vein
2. Left common carotid artery
3. Thymus gland
4. Arch of the aorta
5. Diaphragm
6. Right brachiocephalic vein
7. Subclavian artery and vein
8. 1st rib
9. Superior vena cava

FUN FACTS

1) The heart beats about 100,000 times per day, pumping blood throughout the entire body.
2) The human heart is roughly the size of a clenched fist.
3) The distinctive "lub-dub" sound of the heartbeat is produced by the closing of heart valves

ARTERIES OF THE UPPER LIMB AND BRAIN

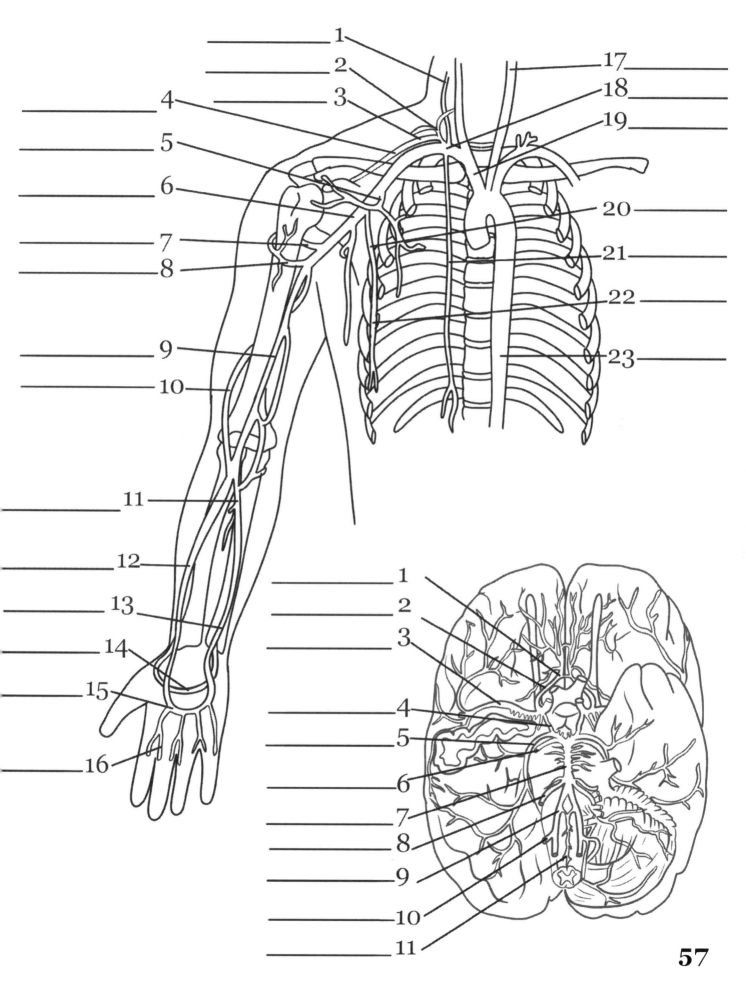

ARTERIES OF THE UPPER LIMB AND BRAIN

Upper Limb

1. Vertebral artery
2. Thyrocervical trunk
3. Costocervical trunk
4. Suprascapular artery
5. Thoraco-acromial artery
6. Axillary artery
7. Posterior circumflex humeral artery
8. Anterior circumflex humeral artery
9. Brachial artery
10. Deep brachial artey
11. Common interosseous artery
12. Radial artery
13. Ulnar artery
14. Deep palmar arch artery
15. Superficial palmar arch artery
16. Digitalis artery
17. Common carotid arteries
18. Subclavian artery
19. Brachiocephalic trunk
20. Suprascapular artery
21. Internal thoracic artery
22. Lateral thoracic artery
23. Descending aorta

Brain

1. Anterior communicating artery
2. Anterior cerebral artery
3. Middle cerebral artery
4. Posterior communicating artery
5. Posterior cerebral artery
6. Superior cerebellar artery artery
7. Basilar artery artery
8. Anterior inferior cerebellar artery
9. Vertebral artery
10. Posterior inferior cerebellar artery

11. Anterior spinal artery

ARTERIES OF THE HEAD AND NECK

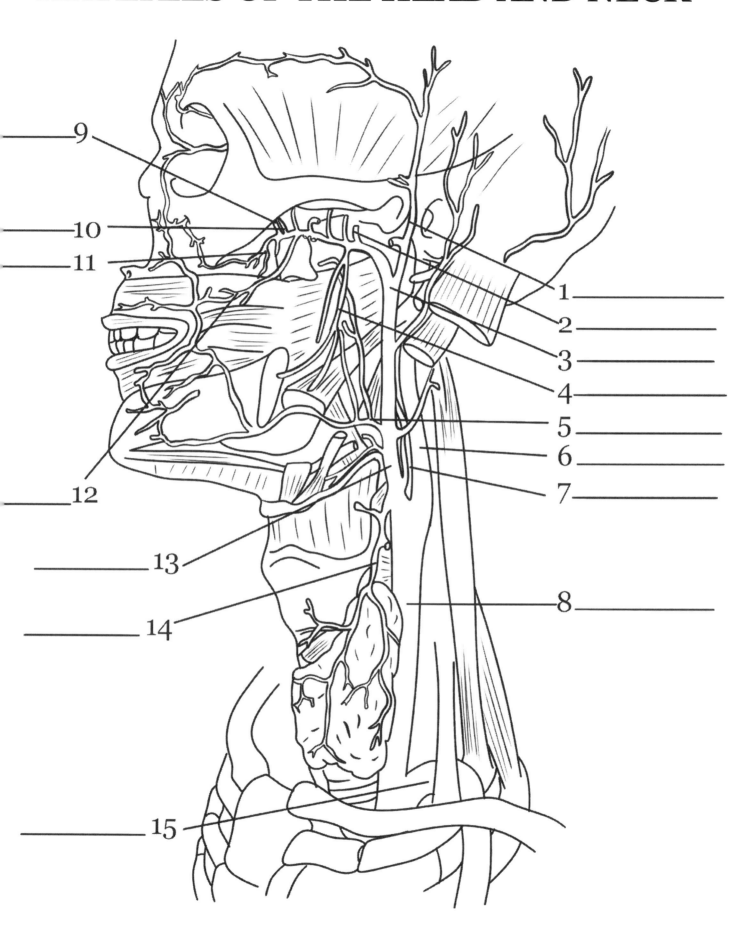

ARTERIES OF THE HEAD AND NECK

1. Superficial temporal artery
2. Middle meningeal artery
3. Maxillary artery
4. Inferior alveolar artery
5. Facial artery
6. Internal carotid artery
7. Ascending pharyngeal artery
8. Common carotid artery
9. Infra-orbital artery
10. Sphenopalatine artery
11. Superior alveolar artery
12. Buccal artery
13. External carotid artery
14. Superior thyroid artery
15. Subclavian artery

FUN FACT

The carotid and temporal arteries are common pulse points in the head and neck. These are locations where you can feel your pulse, reflecting the rhythmic beating of the heart

ARTERIES AND VEINS OF THE LOWER LIMB

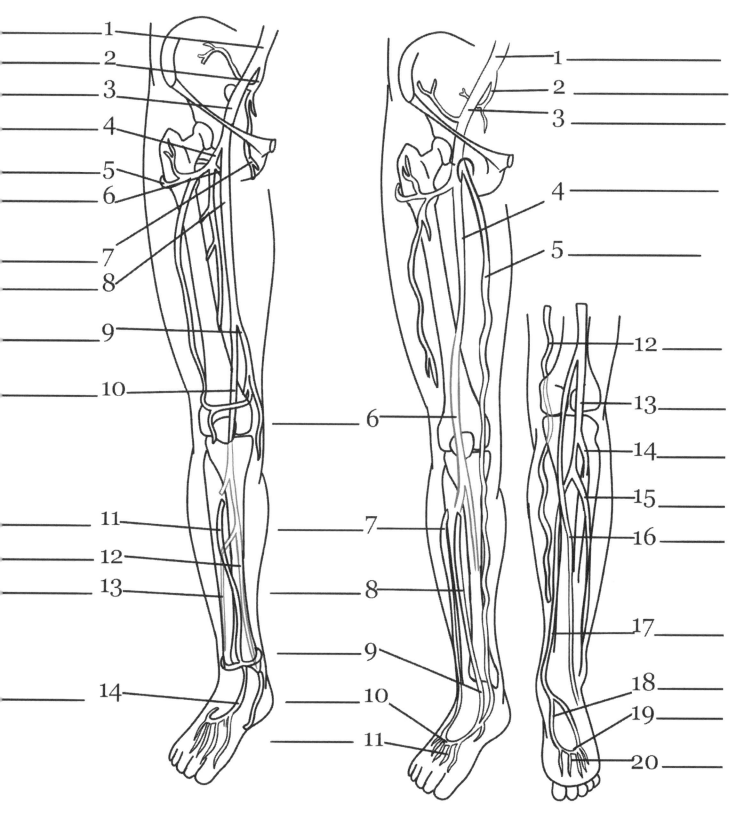

Arteries

Veins

ARTERIES AND VEINS OF THE LOWER LIMB

Arteries

1. Common iliac artery
2. Internal iliac artery
3. External iliac artery
4. Deep femoral artery
5. Lateral circumflex femoral artery
6. Medial circumflex femoral artery
7. Obturator artery
8. Femoral artery
9. Adductor hiatus
10. Popliteal artery
11. Anterior tibial artery
12. Posterior tibial artery
13. Fibular artery
14. Dorsalis pedis artery

Veins

1. Common iliac vein
2. Internal iliac vein
3. External iliac vein
4. Femoral vein
5. Great saphenous vein
6. Popliteal vein
7. Peroneal vein
8. Anterior tibial vein
9. Dorsalis pedis vein
10. Dorsalis pedis arch
11. Metatarsal veins
12. Great saphenous vein
13. Popliteal vein
14. Anterior tibial vein
15. Peroneal vein
16. Small saphenous vein
17. Posterior tibial vein
18. Plantar veins
19. Plantar arch
20. Digital veins

FUN FACT

The great saphenous vein is one of the longest veins in the human body. The calf muscle pump, including the great saphenous vein, acts like a "second heart" by contracting during movement, helping pump blood back to the hear

THORACO-ABDOMINAL ARTERIES

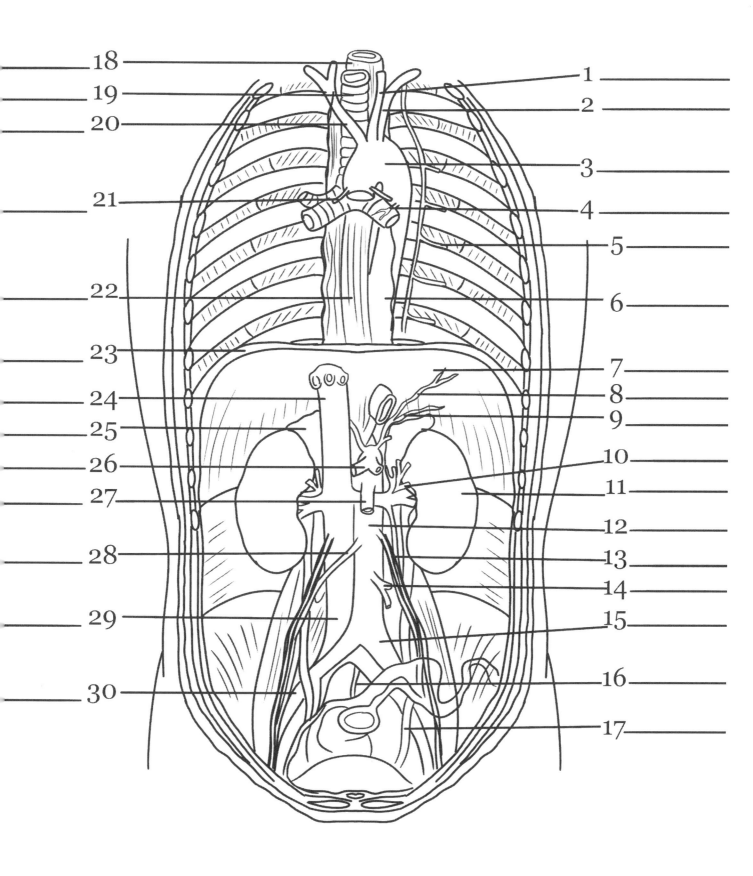

THORACO-ABDOMINAL ARTERIES

1. Left common carotid artery
2. Left subclavian artery
3. Aorta
4. Bronchial artery
5. Anterior intercostal artery
6. Aorta
7. Esophagus
8. Inferior phrenic artery
9. Suprarenal artery
10. Renal artery
11. Kidney
12. Aorta
13. Gonadol artery
14. Inferior mesenteric
15. Common iliac artery
16. Median sacral artery
17. Internal iliac artery
18. Esophagus
19. Trachea
20. Brachiocephalic trunk
21. Coronary arteries
22. Esophagus
23. Diaphragm
24. Inferior vena cava
25. Suprarenal gland
26. Celiac trunk artery
27. Superior mesenteric artery
28. Gonadal artery
29. Inferior vena cava
30. External iliac artery

GASTRO-INTESTINAL TRACT ARTERIES

A.

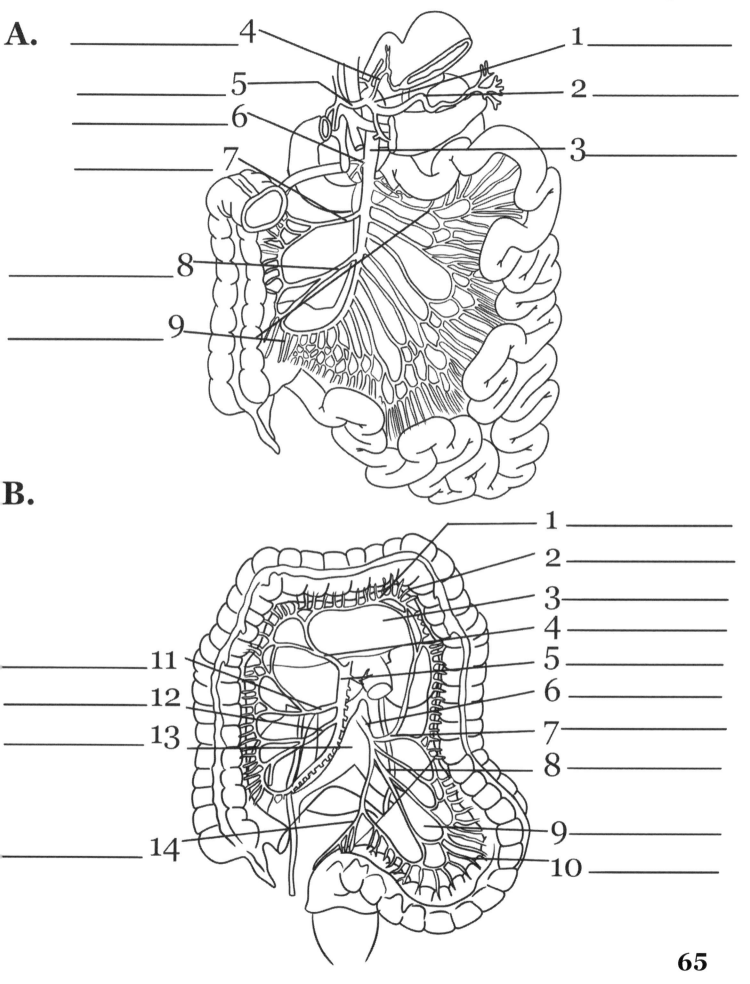

B.

GASTRO-INTESTINAL TRACT ARTERIES

A.

1. Celiac trunk
2. Splenic branch of the celiac trunk
3. Superior mesenteric artery
4. Left gastric branch of the celiac trunk
5. Common hepatic branch of the celiac trunk
6. Middle colic branch of the SMA
7. Right colic branch of the SMA
8. Ileocolic branch of the SMA
9. Jejunal and intestinal ileal arteries

B.

1. Marginal artery
2. Straight arteries
3. Transverse mesocolon
4. Middle colic branch of the SMA
5. Superior mesenteric artery (SMA)
6. Inferior mesenteric artery
7. Left colic branch of the inferior mesenteric artery
8. Sigmoid branches of the IMA
9. Sigmoid mesocolon
10. Straight arteries
11. Right colic branch of the SMA
12. Ileocolic branch of the SMA
13. Aorta
14. Superior rectal branch of the IMA

VEINS OF THE THORAX

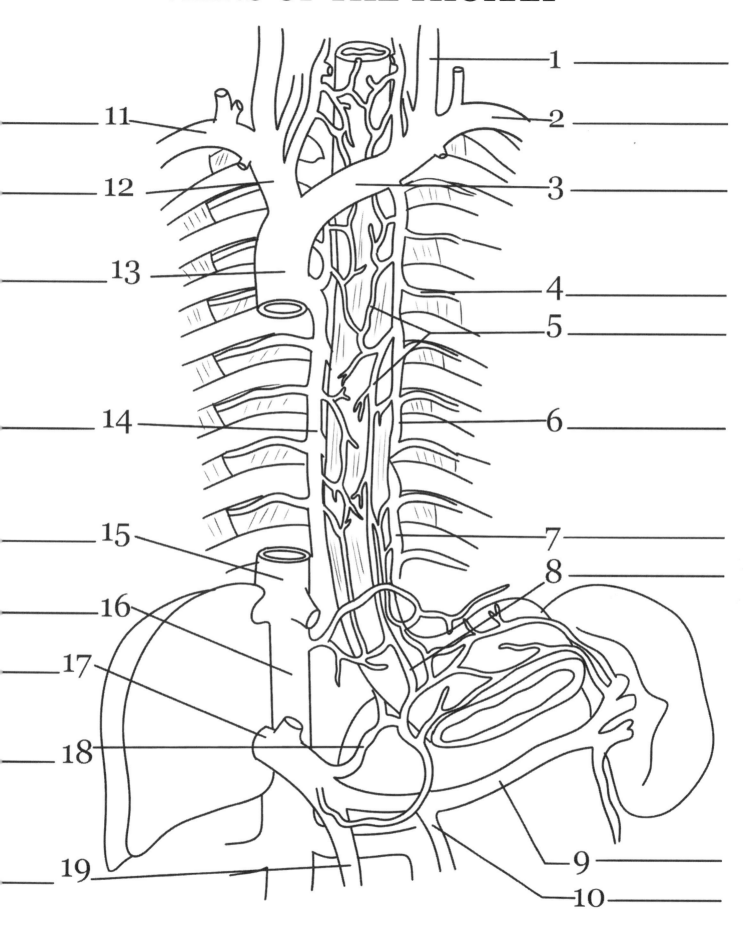

1 —————————————

2 —————————————

3 —————————————

4 —————————————

5 —————————————

6 —————————————

7 —————————————

8 —————————————

9 —————————————

10 —————————————

————————— 11

————————— 12

————————— 13

————————— 14

————————— 15

————————— 16

————————— 17

————————— 18

————————— 19

VEINS OF THE THORAX

1. Internal jugular vein
2. Subclavian vein
3. Left brachiocephalic vein
4. Posterior intercostal vein
5. Esophageal veins
6. Accessory hemi-azygos vein
7. Hemi-azygos vein
8. Esophageal branches of left gastric vein
9. Splenic vein
10. Inferior mesenteric vein
11. Subclavian vein
12. Right brachiocephalic
13. Superior vena cava
14. Azygos vein
15. Inferior vena cava (cut)
16. Inferior vena cava
17. Hepatic portal vein
18. Left gastric vein
19. Superior mesenteric vei

VEINS OF THE UPPER LIMB AND ABDOMEN

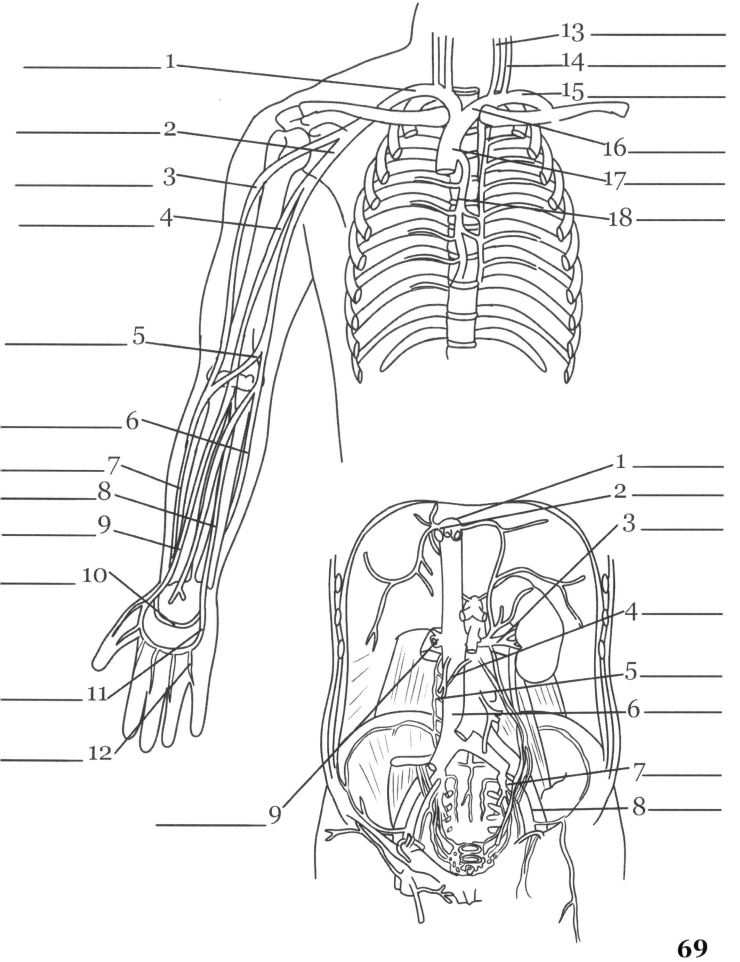

VEINS OF THE UPPER LIMB AND ABDOMEN

Upper limb

1. Subclavian vein
2. Axillary vein
3. Cephalic vein
4. Brachial vein
5. Median cubital vein
6. Radial vein
7. Cephalic vein
8. Ulnar vein
9. Radial vein
10. Deep palmar venous arch
11. Superficial palmar venous arch
12. Digital veins
13. Internal jugular vein
14. External jugular vein
15. Left subclavian vein
16. Brachiocephalic veins
17. Superior vena cava
18. Azygos vein

Abdomen

1. Hepatic vein
2. Inferior phrenic vein
3. Renal vein
4. Right and left gonadal veins
5. Ascending lumbar veins
6. Inferior vena cava
7. Internal iliac vein
8. External iliac vein

> **FUN FACT**
> The portal vein is a major vein that carries nutrient-rich blood from the digestive organs (stomach, intestines, spleen, and pancreas) to the liver. It plays a key role in nutrient processing and metabolism
> The cephalic vein is a prominent superficial vein that travels along the lateral (outer) aspect of the arm. It is often used for venipuncture and is visible when looking at the forearm

NEONATAL CIRCULATION

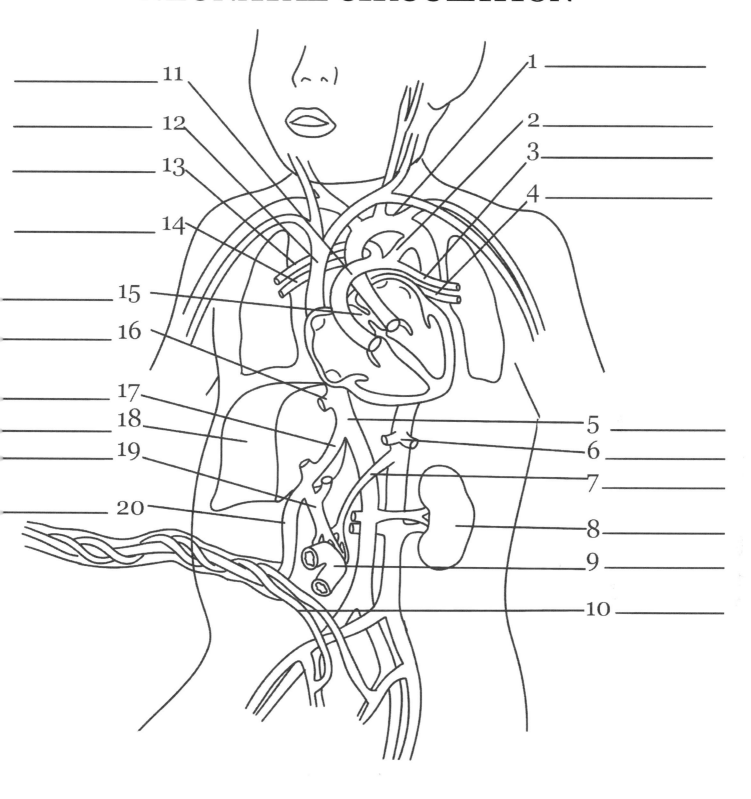

NEONATAL CIRCULATION

1. Aorta
2. Umbilical vein
3. Left pulmonary artery
4. Left pulmonary vein
5. Inferior vena cava
6. Celiac trunk
7. Superior mesenteric artery
8. Kidney
9. Gut
10. Umbilical arteries
11. Pulmonary trunk
12. Superior vena cava
13. Right pulmonary artery
14. Right pulmonary vein
15. Foramen ovale
16. Hepatic vein
17. Ductus venosus
18. Liver
19. Hepatic vein
20. Umbilical vein

NASAL CAVITY AND PARANASAL SINUSES

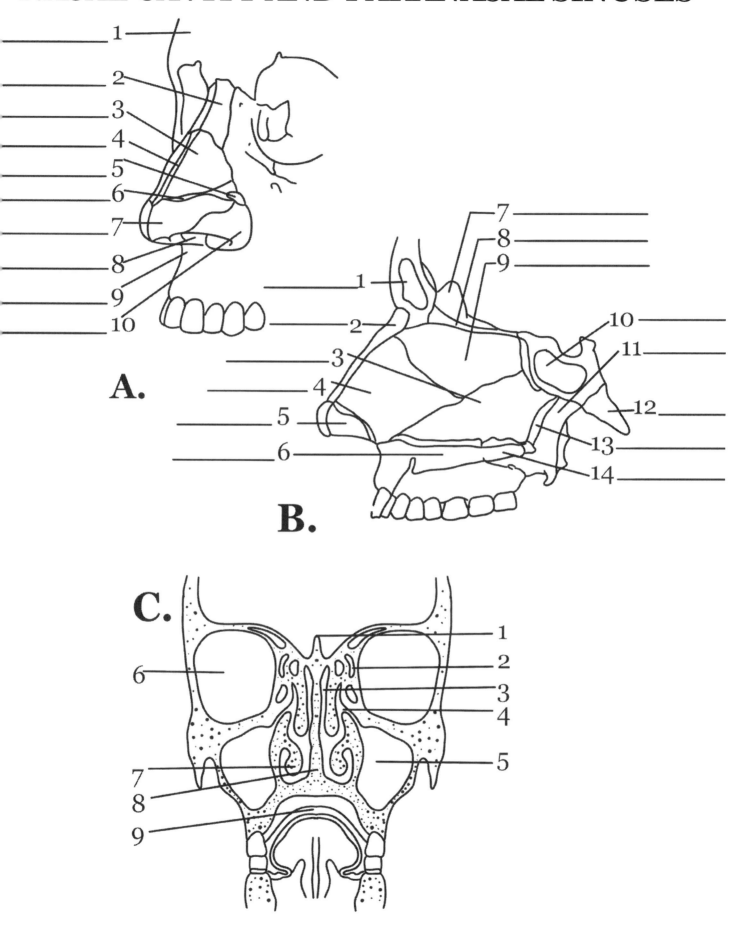

A.

B.

C.

NASAL CAVITY AND PARANASAL SINUSES

A.
1. Frontal bone
2. Nasal bones
3. Lateral processes of the septal cartilage
4. Septal Cartilage
5. Minor alar cartilage
6. Accessory nasal cartilage
7. Major alar cartilages
8. Nasal septal cartilage
9. Anterior nasal spine of maxilla
10. Alar fibrofatty tissue

B.
1. Frontal Sinus
2. Nasal bone
3. Vomer
4. Septal Cartilage
5. Major alar cartilages
6. Palatine process of maxilla
7. Crista galli
8. Cribriform plate
9. Perpendicular plate of the ethmoid
10. Sphenoidal sinus
11. Medial plate of pterygoid process
12. Basilar part of occipital bone
13. Perpendicular plate
14. Palatine Horizontal plate

C.
1. Crista galli
2. Ethmoid Air cells
3. Nasal cavities
4. Opening of maxillary sinus
5. Maxillary sinus
6. Orbit
7. Inferior nasal concha
8. Vomer
9. Oral Cavity

FUN FACT
A sneeze can travel at speeds of up to 100 miles per hour (160 km/h). It's a rapid expulsion of air meant to clear the respiratory system of irritants. The average person takes about 12 to 20 breaths per minute. This rhythmic pattern is regulated by the respiratory center in the brain

TRACHEA AND LUNGS

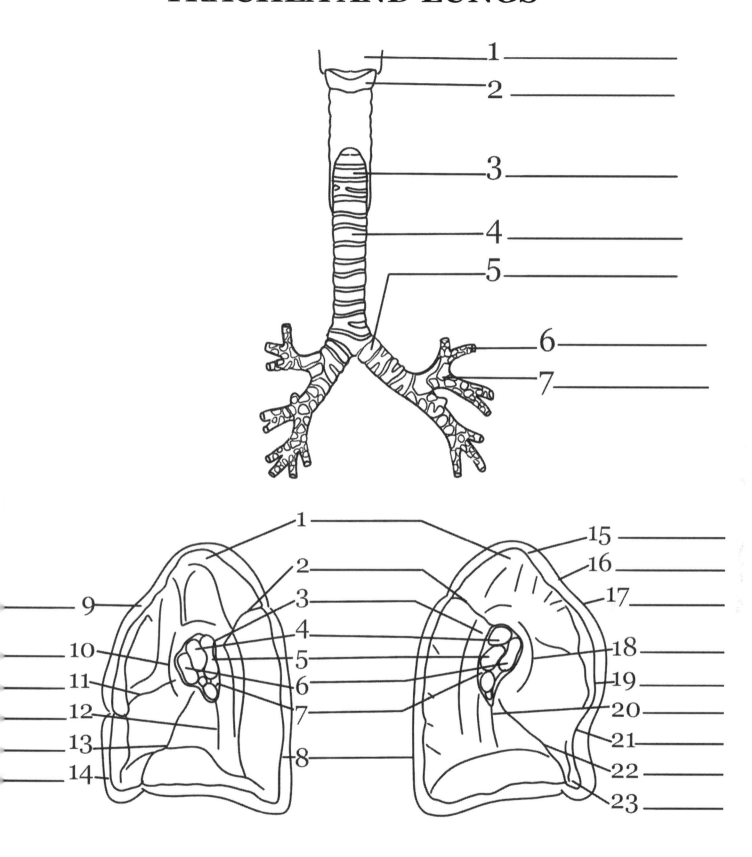

1 _____

2 _____

3 _____

4 _____

5 _____

6 _____

7 _____

9 _____

10 _____

11 _____

12 _____

13 _____

14 _____

15 _____

16 _____

17 _____

18 _____

19 _____

20 _____

21 _____

22 _____

23 _____

8 _____

TRACHEA AND LUNGS

Trachea

1. Thyroid cartilage
2. Cricoid cartilage
3. Trachea cartilages
4. Trachea
5. Primary main bronchi
6. Tertiary bronch
7. Secondary branch

Lungs

1. Apex
2. Oblique fissure
3. Pleura
4. Pulmonary artery
5. Bronchus
6. Pulmonary veins
7. Bronchopulmonary lymph nodes
8. Inferior lobe
9. Superior lobe
10. Hilum
11. Horizontal fissure
12. Pulmonary ligament
13. Oblique fissure
14. Middle lobe
15. Cupula pleura
16. Patietal pleura
17. Superior lobe
18. Hilum
19. Visceral pleura
20. Pulmonary ligament
21. Cardiac notch
22. Oblique fissure
23. Lingula

FUN FACT

1) The inner lining of the trachea is covered with mucus and tiny hair-like structures called cilia. This combination helps trap and move particles, such as dust and bacteria, away from the lungs

2) The Heimlich maneuver, a first aid technique used to help someone choking, involves applying abdominal pressure to force air out of the lungs through the trachea, expelling the obstructing object

GASTRO-INTESTINAL SYSTEM OVERVIEW

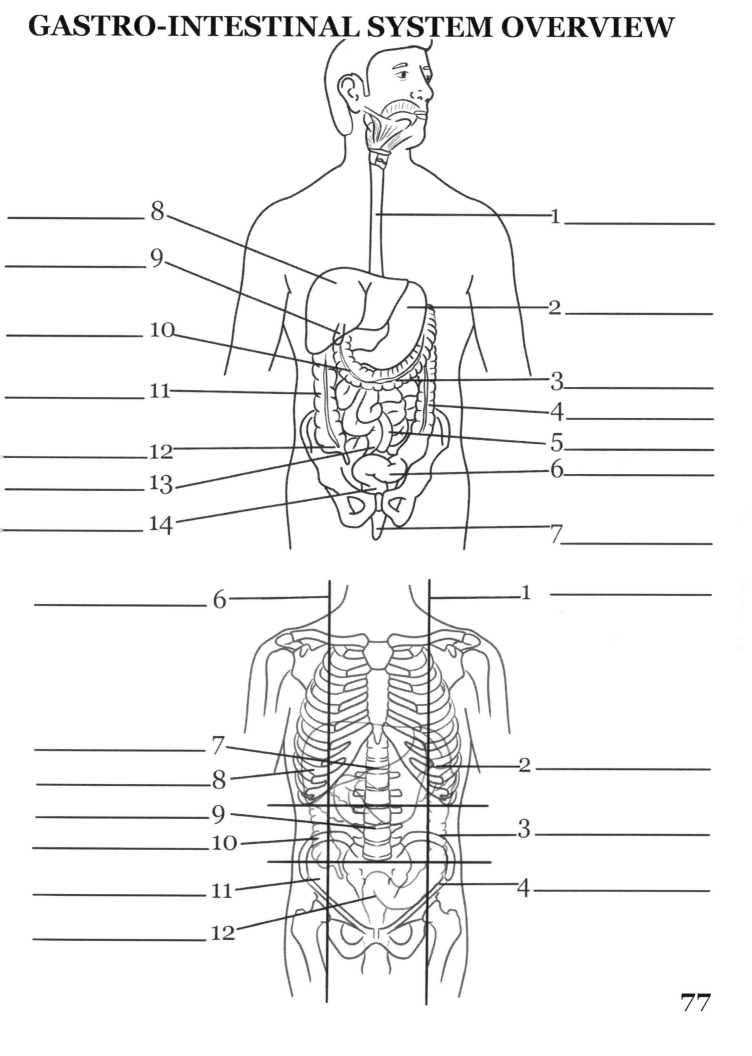

8

9

10

11

12

13

14

1

2

3

4

5

6

7

6

1

7

8

9

10

11

12

2

3

4

77

GASTRO-INTESTINAL SYSTEM OVERVIEW

A

1. Esophagus
2. Stomach
3. Transverse colon
4. Descending colon
5. Jejunum
6. Sigmoid colon
7. Anal canal
8. Liver
9. Gallbladder
10. Duodenum
11. Ascending colon
12. Cecum
13. Ileum
14. Rectum

B

1. Left midclavicular line
2. Left hypochondriac region
3. Left Lumbar region
4. Left Inguinal region
5. Right midclavicular line
6. Right midclavicular line
7. Epigastric region
8. Right hypochondriac region
9. Umbilical region
10. Right lumbar region
11. Right inguinal region
12. Pubic hypogastic region

> **FUN FACT**
> 1) The phrase "gut feeling" isn't just a figure of speech. The gut has its nervous system called the enteric nervous system, often referred to as the "second brain," which can influence mood and emotions.
> 2) Just like fingerprints, everyone's gut microbiota is unique. No two individuals have the exact same combination of microorganisms in their digestive systems

ORAL CAVITY, PHARYNX AND ESOPHAGUS

A.

B.

C.

ORAL CAVITY, PHARYNX AND ESOPHAGUS

A.
1. Transverse palatine folds
2. Palatine raphe
3. Hard palate
4. Uvula
5. Palatine tonsil
6. Tongue

B.
1. Pharyngeal tonsil
2. Nasal septum
3. Parotid gland
4. Uvula
5. Epiglottis
6. Laryngeal inlet
7. Esophagus
8. Trachea
9. Choanae
10. Soft palate
11. Palatine tonsil
12. Piriform fossa

C.
1. Cervical part of esophagus
2. Subclavian artery
3. Esophagus
4. Common carotid artery
5. Arch of aorta
6. Thoracic (descending) aorta
7. Esophageal branches of thoracic aorta
8. Diaphragm
9. Stomach
10. Subclavian artery
11. Brachiocephalic trunk
12. Trachea
13. Esophagus
14. Thoracic part of esophagus
15. Abdominal part of esophagus

80

> **FUN FACT**
>
> 1) Adults typically have 32 teeth, each serving a specific purpose. Incisors are for cutting, canines for tearing, and molars for grinding and crushing food.
> 2) The esophagus does not produce digestive enzymes. Its primary function is to transport food to the stomach

PERITONEAL CAVITY AND STOMACH

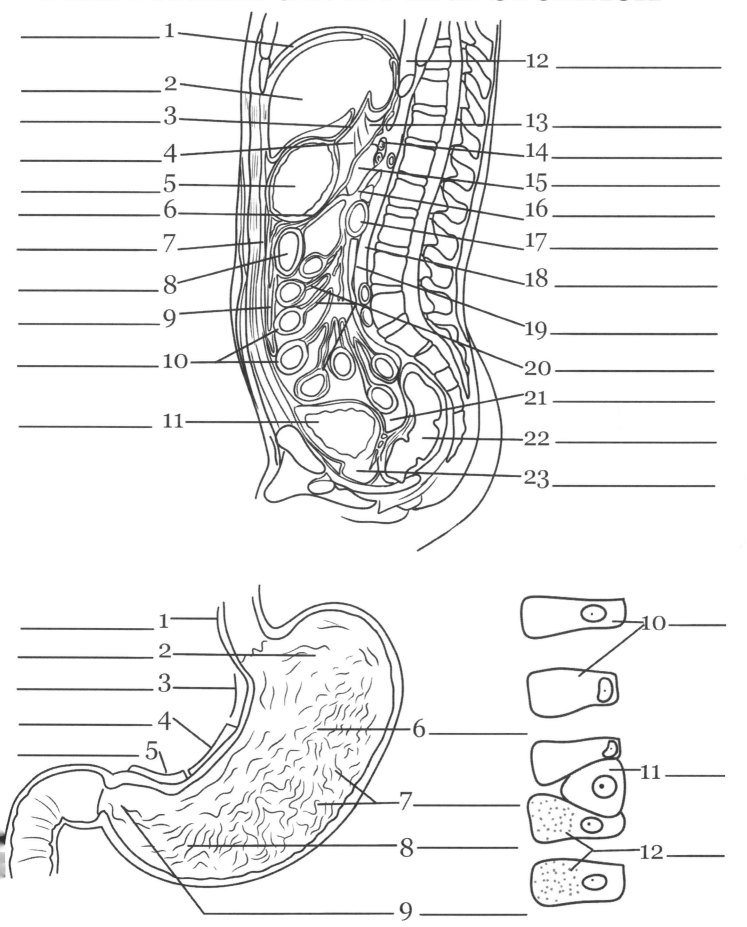

PERITONEAL CAVITY AND STOMACH

Peritoneal Cavity

1. Diaphragm
2. Liver
3. Lesser omentum
4. lesser sac
5. Stomach
6. Transverse mesocolon
7. Parietal peritoneum (of anterior abdominal wall)
8. Transverse colon
9. Greater omentum
10. Small intestine
11. Urinary bladder
12. Esophagus
Omental (epiploic) foramen (Winslow)
Celiac trunk
Pancreas
Superior mesenteric artery
Inferior (horizontal, or 3rd) part of duodenum
Abdominal aorta
Parietal peritoneum
20. Mesentery of the small intestine
21. Rectovesical pouch
22. Rectum
23. Prostate gland

Stomach

1. Cardiac zone
2. Fundus
3. Fundic zone
4. Transitional zone
5. Pyloric zone
6. Body of stomach
7. Rugae
8. Pyloric antrum
9. Pyloric canal
10. Mucous neck cells
11. Parietal cells
12. Chief cells

SMALL AND LARGE INTESTINE

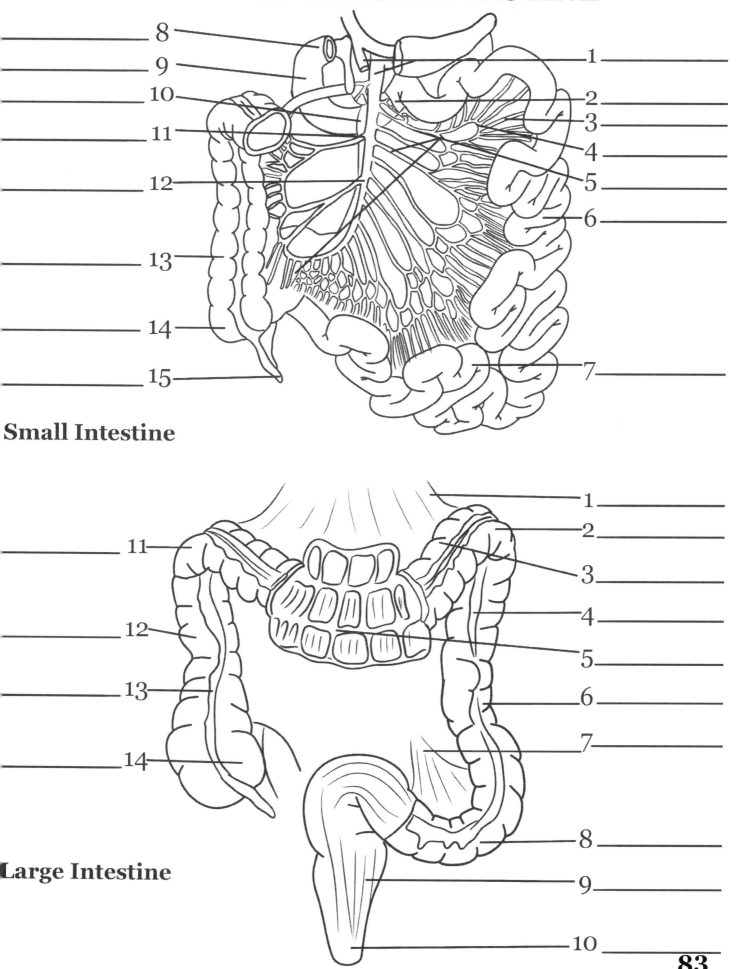

Small Intestine

Large Intestine

SMALL AND LARGE INTESTINE

Small Intestine

1. Superior mesenteric artery and vein
2. Fourth (ascending) part of the duodenum
3. Straight arteries
4. Anastomotic loops
5. Jejunal and ileal arteries
6. Jejunum
7. Ileum
8. First part of the duodenum
9. Second (descending) part of the duodenum
10. Third (horizontal) part of the duodenum
11. Right colic artery
12. Ileocolic artery
13. Ascending colon
14. Cecum
15. Appendix

Large Intestine

1. Transverse mesocolon
2. Splenic flexure
3. Transverse colon
4. Taenia coli
5. Semilunar folds
6. Descending colon
7. Sigmoid mesocolon
8. Sigmoid colon
9. Rectum
10. Anal canal
11. Hepatic flexure
12. Ascending colon
13. Taenia coli
14. Cecum

FUN FACT

The small intestine is much longer than the large intestine. It's coiled within the abdomen and measures about 20 feet in length on average.

The large intestine is home to a vast community of beneficial bacteria known as gut microbiota

LIVER AND GALL BLADDER

5

1

6

2

3

4

7

15

8

16

9

17

10

18

11

12

19

13

20

14

21

1

2

3

4

5

6

13

7

14

8

15

9

16

10

17

11

12

LIVER AND GALL BLADDER

Liver

1. Coronary ligament
2. Left lobe of liver
3. Falciform ligament
4. Ligamentum teres
5. Diaphragm
6. Right lobe of liver
7. Gallbladder
8. Inferior vena cava
9. Bare area
10. Hepatic veins
11. Common bile duct
12. Cystic duct
13. Gallbladder
14. Right lobe
15. Ligamentum venosum
16. Caudate lobe
17. Hepatic portal vein
18. Hepatic artery proper
19. Falciform ligament
20. Round ligament of the liver
21. Quadrate lobe

Gallbladder

1. Liver
2. Common hepatic duct
3. Cystic duct
4. Proper hepatic artery
5. Common bile duct
6. Right gastric artery
7. Gastroduodenal artery
8. Anterior layer of lesser omentum
9. Duodenum
10. Common bile duct
11. Pancreas
12. Colon
13. Common hepatic duct
14. Cystic duct
15. Common bile duct
16. Gallbladder
17. Main pancreatic duct

FUN FACT

The liver is a metabolic powerhouse, involved in processing nutrients from the food you eat. It regulates glucose levels, stores vitamins and minerals, and helps convert food into energy.he gallbladder is a small, pear-shaped organ that stores and concentrates bile produced by the liver. Bile is released into the small intestine to aid in the digestion of fats

URINARY SYSTEM

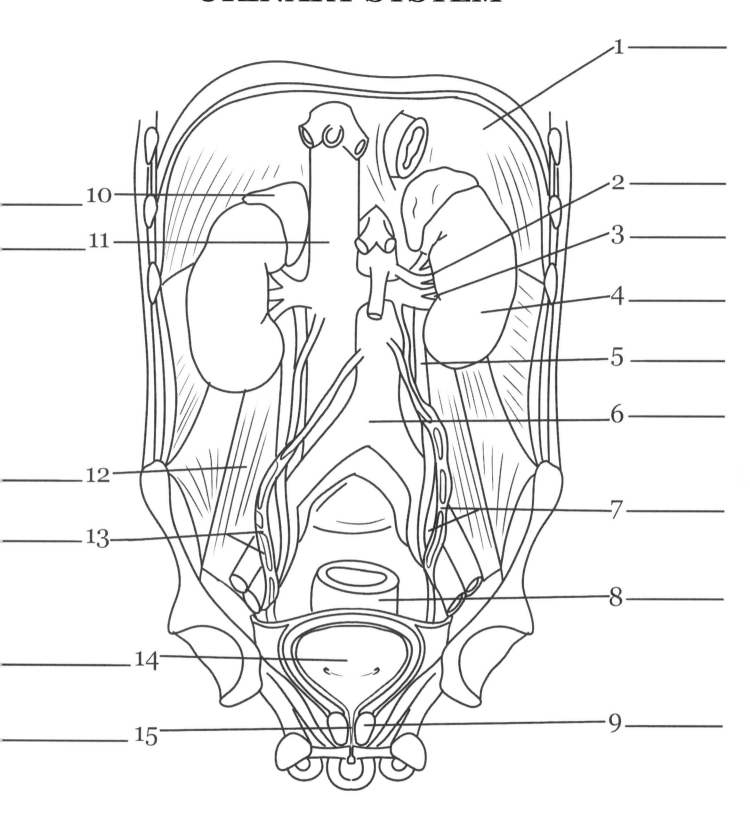

1

2

3

4

5

6

7

8

9

10

11

12

13

14

15

URINARY SYSTEM

1. Diaphragm
2. Renal artery
3. Renal vein
4. Kidney
5. Ureter
6. Aorta
7. Left Testicular artery and vein
8. Rectum
9. Prostate gland
10. Adrenal gland
11. Inferior vena cava
12. Psoas major muscle
13. Right Testicular artery and vein
14. Urinary bladder
15. Urethra

KIDNEYS

8   1
    2
    3
9   4
    5
10   6
    7
11

12   22   29
13   23   30
14   24   31
15   32
16   25   26   33
17
18   27
19   28
20
21

89

KIDNEYS

1. Left suprarenal gland
2. Kidney
3. Renal artery
4. Renal vein
5. Superior mesenteric artery
6. Left Ureter
7. Abdominal aorta
8. Right suprarenal gland
9. Renal artery
10. Inferior vena cava
11. Right ureter
12. Fibrous capsule
13. Renal cortex
14. Renal pyramids
15. Minor calices
16. Renal papilla
17. Base of pyramid
18. Major calices
19. Renal pelvis
20. Minor calices
21. Ureter
22. Superior segmental artery
23. Anterior superior segmental artery
24. Inferior superficial artery
25. Renal artery
26. Anterior inferior segmental artery
27. Posterior segmental arteries
28. Inferior segmental artery
29. Renal cortex
30. Renal pyramids
31. Interlobar arteries
32. Arcuate arteries
33. Cortical radiate

FUN FACT

You have two kidneys, and they act like super-efficient filters for your blood. Each kidney is about the size of a fist and contains around a million nephrons, the tiny units responsible for filtering. Kidneys produce a hormone called renin, which helps regulate blood pressure

NEPHRON

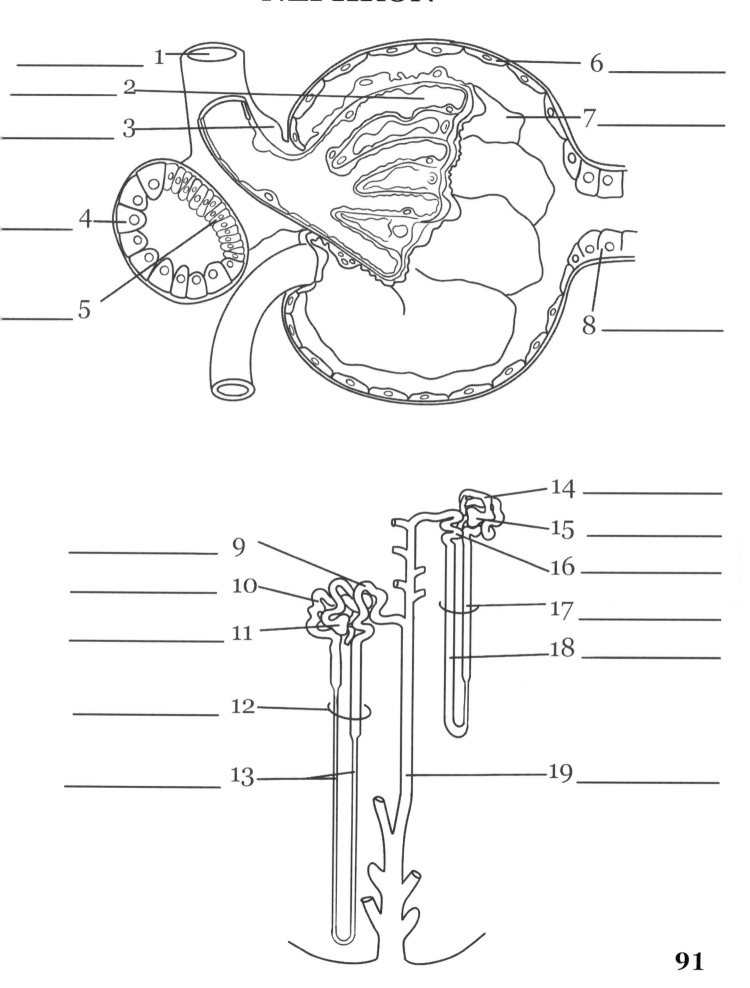

1
2
3
4
5
6
7
8
9
10
11
12
13
14
15
16
17
18
19

NEPHRON

1. Afferent arteriole
2. Endothelium of glomerular capillaries
3. Juxtaglomerular cells
4. Cells lining the Disal convulated tubule
5. Macula densa
6. Bowman's capsule
7. Podocytes
8. Epithelium of Proximal convoluted tubule
9. Distal convolution
10. Proximal tubule
11. Juxtamedullary glomerulus
12. Loop of Henle
13. Thin descending and ascending loop of Henle
14. Proximal convulated tubule
15. Cortical glomerulus
16. Distal ascending loop of Henle
17. Loop of Henle
18. Distal ascending loop of Henle
19. Collecting duct

FUN FACT
The nephron is the functional unit of the kidney, responsible for filtering and regulating the composition of blood. Each kidney contains around a million nephrons. Glucose and certain ions, are retained and returned to the bloodstream, while waste products are efficiently directed to form urine

URINARY BLADDER AND URETHRA

Female Urethra

Male Urethra

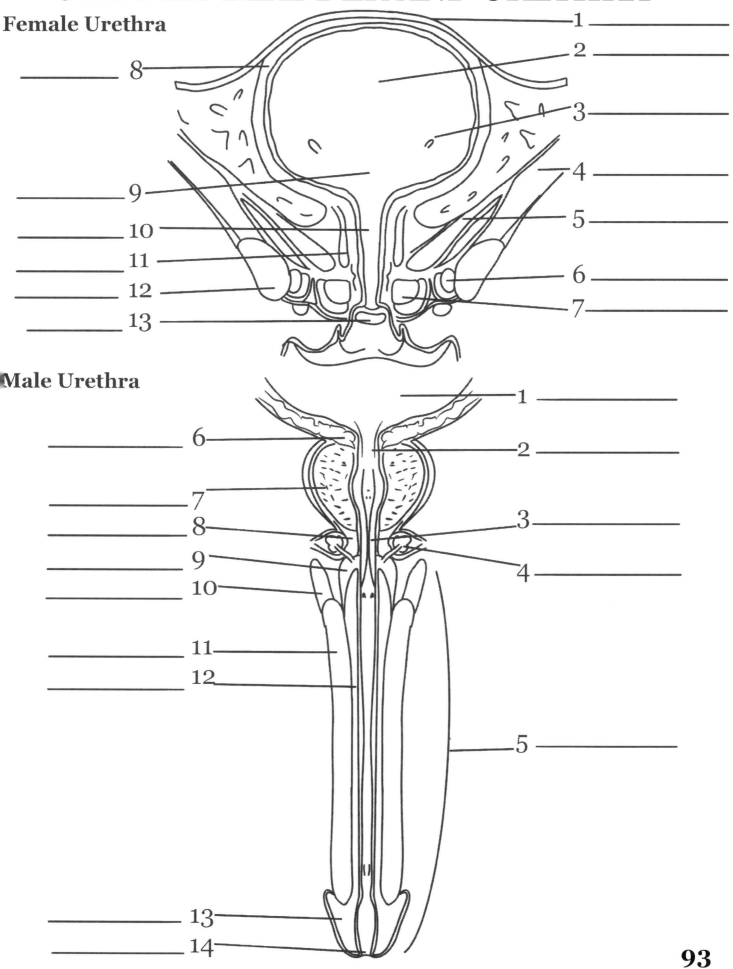

URINARY BLADDER AND URETHRA

Female Urethra

1. Peritoneum
2. Fundus of bladder
3. Left ureteric orifice
4. Obturator internus muscle
5. Levator ani muscle
6. Crus of clitoris
7. Bulb of vestibul
8. Detrusor muscle of the female bladder wall
9. Trigone of the female bladder
10. Female urethra
11. Sphincter urethrae muscle in the female
12. Inferior pubic ramus
13. Vagina

Male Urethra

1. Trigone of the male bladder
2. Prostatic urethra
3. Membranous urethra
4. Bulbo-urethra gland
5. Spongy urethra
6. Internal urethral sphincter
7. Prostate
8. Spongy urethra
9. Bulb of penis
10. Crus of penis
11. Corpus cavernosum
12. Corpus spongiosum

FUN FACT

The bladder is an impressive organ with remarkable stretching abilities. When it's empty, the bladder resembles a collapsed balloon. As it fills with urine, it expands and stretches. An adult human bladder can typically hold about 400 to 600 milliliters of urine

FEMALE REPRODUCTIVE SYSTEM

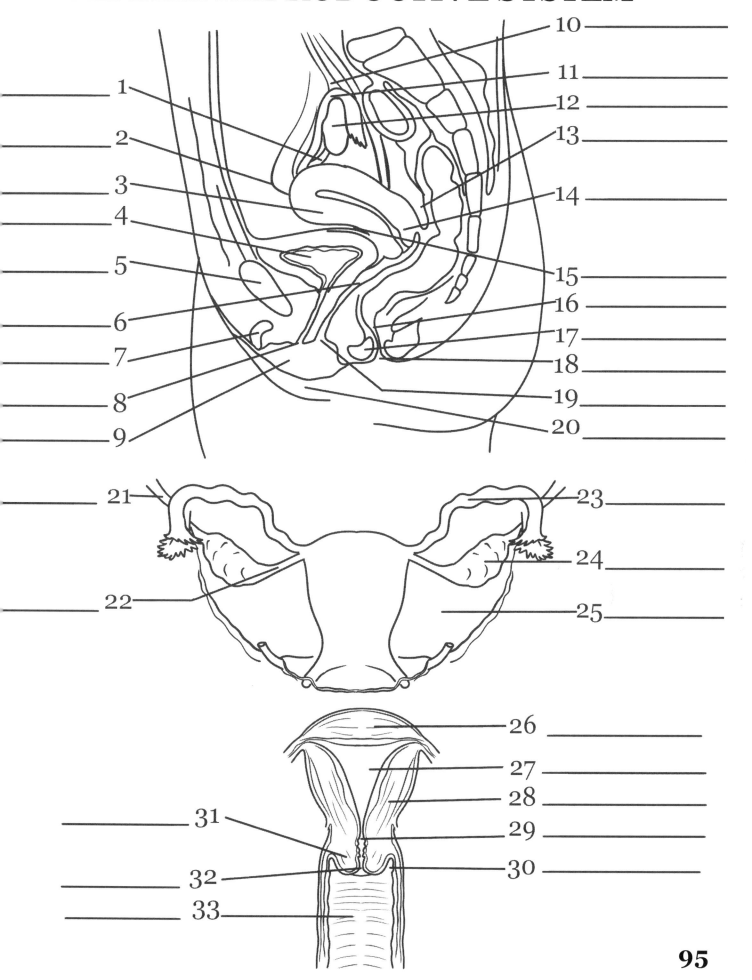

95

FEMALE REPRODUCTIVE SYSTEM

1. Ligament of ovary
2. Round ligament of uterus
3. Uterus
4. Urinary bladder
5. Pubic symphysis
6. Vagina
7. Clitoris
8. Urethral opening
9. Labia minora
10. Suspensory ligament of ovary
11. Uterine tube
12. Ovary
13. Recto-uterine pouch
14. Cervix of uterus
15. Vesico-uterine pouch
16. Anal canal
17. External anal sphincter
18. Anus
19. Vaginal opening
20. Labia majora
21. Suspensory ligament of ovary
22. Ligament of ovary
23. Uterine tube
24. Ovary
25. Broad ligament
26. Fundus of the uterus
27. Uterine cavity
28. Body of the uterus
29. Internal opening

30. Vaginal fornix
31. Cervix of the uterus
32. External opening
33. Vagina

FUN FACT

Females are born with all the eggs they'll ever have. At birth, a baby girl already carries all the immature eggs she'll need for her reproductive life. The number decreases over time At birth, a female may have around 1 to 2 million eggs, but by the onset of puberty, this number reduces to a few hundred thousands

BREAST AND OVARY

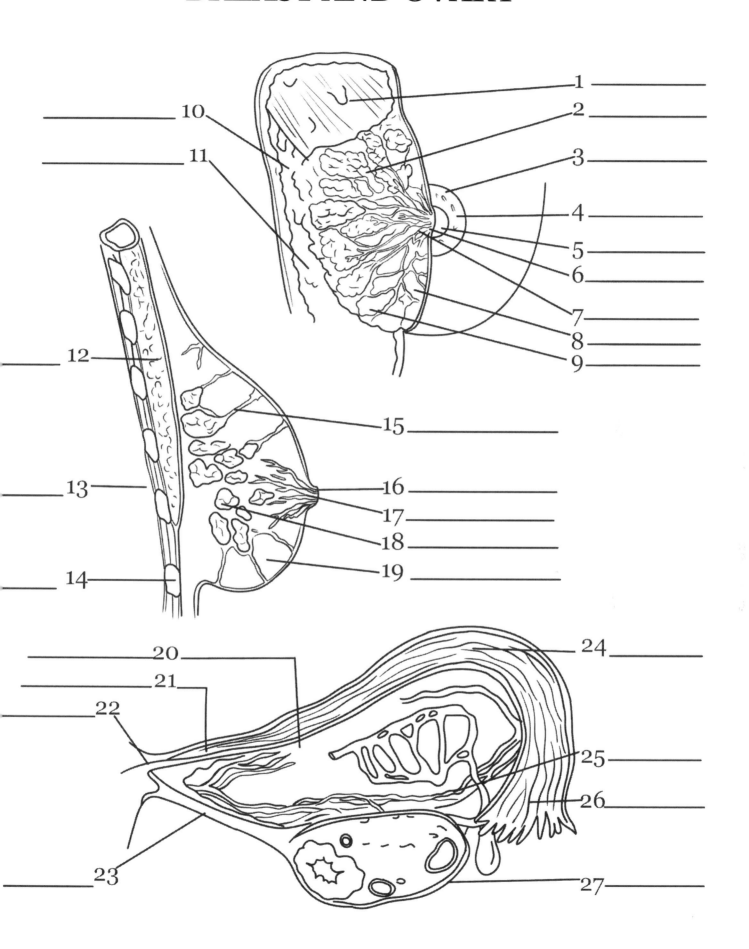

1 _____

10 _____

11 _____

2 _____

3 _____

4 _____

5 _____

6 _____

7 _____

8 _____

9 _____

12 _____

13 _____

14 _____

15 _____

16 _____

17 _____

18 _____

19 _____

20 _____

21 _____

22 _____

23 _____

24 _____

25 _____

26 _____

27 _____

BREAST AND OVARY

1. Pectoralis major muscle
2. Suspensory ligaments
3. Areolar glands
4. Areola
5. Nipple
6. Lactiferous ducts
7. Lactiferous sinuses
8. Fatty subcutaneous tissue
9. Gland lobules
10. Serratus anterior muscle
11. External oblique muscle
12. Pectoralis major muscle
13. Lung
14. 6th rib
15. Suspensory ligaments
16. Lactiferous ducts
17. Lactiferous sinuses
18. Gland lobules
19. Fatty subcutaneous tissue
20. Mesosalpinx
21. Isthmus
22. Intramural portion of tube
23. Ovarian ligament
24. Ampulla
25. Ovarian vessels
26. Fimbriated end of the infundibulum
27. Ovary

MALE REPRODUCTIVE SYSTEM

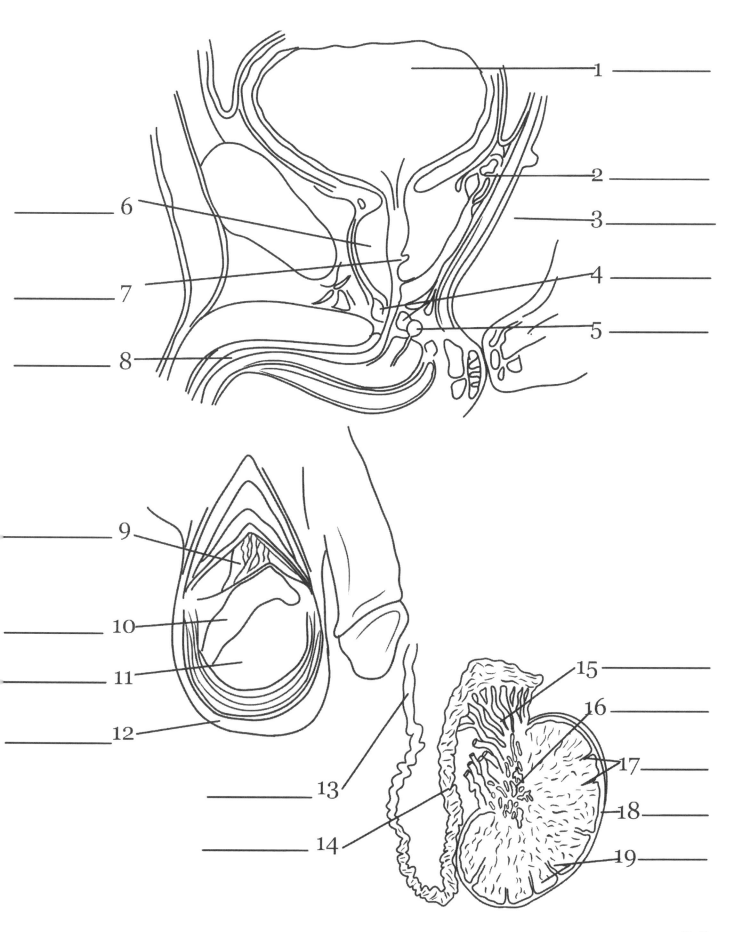

MALE REPRODUCTIVE SYSTEM

1. Urinary bladder
2. Seminal vesicle
3. Rectum
4. Sphincter urethrae muscle
5. Bulbo-urethral glands
6. Prostate gland
7. Opening of ejaculatory duct
8. Urethra
9. Ductus deferens
10. Epididymis
11. Testis
12. Skin of scrotum
13. Ductus deferens
14. Epididymis
15. Efferent ductules
16. Rete testis
17. Septa
18. Tunica albigans
19. Lobules

FUN FACT

The male reproductive system produces tiny, fast swimmers! Sperm, the reproductive cells, can move at an impressive speed of about 1 to 4 millimeters per minute. It's like a miniature race inside the body, where only the fastest can reach the finish line and contribute to the creation of new life

CONCLUSION

As we close the pages of our Human Anatomy Coloring Book, we reflect on a journey that was as enlightening as it was vibrant. Through each chapter, you've explored the wonders of the human body, from the intricate network of bones and muscles to the delicate interplay of the nervous and circulatory systems. By coloring and learning, you've transformed complex anatomical concepts into vivid, memorable experiences.

Now, with this rich tapestry of knowledge at your fingertips, you're equipped to apply what you've learned in practical, meaningful ways. Whether it's enhancing your studies, informing your art, or simply understanding your body better, the insights you've gained here are yours to use and build upon. As you turn the final pages, adorned with your hues and insights, we hope this experience has been as effective for you as it has for us.

If this book has been a valuable companion in your journey of learning and discovery, I encourage you to share your experience. Please consider leaving a review on Amazon to help others embark on this colorful exploration of human anatomy. Your feedback not only supports our work but also guides fellow learners to a resource that combines education with creativity.

Thank you for choosing this journey, and may your path forward be as colorful and enlightening as the pages you've colored.

Made in United States
Troutdale, OR
03/01/2024

18126752R00058